D0108311

a funny thing happened on the way to equality

a funny

thing happened on the way to equality

by

Ellen Peck

Prentice-Hall, Inc.
Englewood Cliffs, New Jersey

Prentice-Hall International, Inc., London
Prentice-Hall of Australia, Pty. Ltd., Sydney
Prentice-Hall of Canada, Ltd., Toronto
Prentice-Hall of India Private Ltd., New Delhi
Prentice-Hall of Japan, Inc., Tokyo

10 9 8 7 6 5 4 3 2 1

Library of Congress Cataloging in Publication Data

Peck, Ellen
    A funny thing happened on the way to equality.

    1. Feminism—United States. I. Title.
HQ1426.P42 1975   301.41'2   75-15536
ISBN 0-13-345512-2   Dec. 17, 1975

*To Bill and to Don, whose patience
and guidance extended far beyond
the scope of this book*

ACKNOWLEDGEMENT

I wish to thank the women who, over the past year, have shared with me their feelings about the current women's movement, and shared with me also the stories of their experiences with liberation. The stories told in this book are real—as are the women who are the subjects of the stories. However, in all cases, identities have been protected through changes of names, and dates, and circumstance and physical detail, or through the use of composites, in which the experiences of several women have been integrated into one story.

CONTENTS

What Is Feminism?

Once Linda Rollins lived in a large house in Sacramento. Now she lives in a walk-up flat in seedy Venice, California, above an antique shop. Walls bare except for one sheet of tinfoil, bamboo window shades, Christmas tree lights across the ceiling, noisy traffic below, a broken rocker, a broken director's chair, lots of pillows covered with Indian cotton.

The man that Linda lives with isn't like her former husband: he doesn't demand that she wash the vegetables and sweep the floor. Their household contract is a model one, approved by *Ms.* magazine, allowing Linda time for her work as an aspiring writer. (They both care for her seven-year-old daughter.) The adjustment isn't always easy, though. Linda tells this story:

"One day Henry was studying late for exams. I knew he was very tired; and so, even though we do our laundry separately (I at the Fold-and-Fluff, he at the Coin-Op), I, without saying anything, quietly gathered up my laundry *and* his and went to do it.

"I stewed about it all day. I had really lost control. I had forgotten that servility is self-sabotage. In a moment of weakness I had reverted to my former 'housewife' self. I felt so *guilty*. . . ."

A simple act of consideration becomes a guilt-ridden political issue. Linda's life, however, is filled with incidents like this. It's a period of adjustment, she says. *"Feminism,"* she says, *"is learning where to place blame."*

She's figuring it out.

To Linda, feminism may be learning where to place blame, but other women who consider themselves liberated might question that definition, for feminism is multifaceted, lending itself to individual interpretations. To other women, it may be gathering the courage to get a job, or to commit themselves to training for a career, thus achieving new bases for identity and self-respect. To still others, it may mean questioning the total dedication previously given to family and community. To some women, feminism is separatism and man-hating, the movement itself "a fast-moving train that doesn't stop until it gets to the lesbian nation." And to not a few, it is a cause so vital as to be worth total dedication, single-minded commitment—and, not incidentally, daily exhaustion.

Whatever feminism is to individual women, and however it is individually defined, do individual perceptions and definitions grow from some central reality, from the dynamics of that contemporary phenomenon that we have ceased calling Women's Lib and now speak of, more seriously, as *the women's movement*?

The movement *is* real, and anyone who thinks it was a passing fancy would have to have been an ingenious practitioner of media abstinence for the past ten years.

Having survived an initial phase of impulsive and faddish attention-grabbing, the movement may seem less visible now than in the days of supposed undergarment-bonfires, but in fact it is only now becoming serious—and settling in for the long-range purpose of changing our major institutions and social beliefs. It is proclaimed to be, and indeed may be, "the second wave of the most important revolution in history," by Shulamith Firestone and others. Yet its true meaning—after dozens of books, hundreds of conferences, thousands of articles, and millions of private words—remains unclear.

Is the goal to end male supremacy or change female nature? Become closer to men as companions and partners or excise them from the female sphere altogether? Win equal pay for equal work within the existing system or alter that system radically?

Is the movement Marxist? Is it anti-man? Does it seek the destruction or replacement of the nuclear family? Is self-realization possible for women if they continue to live with men?

We all think we know the answers, based on the most recent article, the latest network TV special personal appearance by a leading feminist, or the consensus of our own CR group. Yet the fact that there is no one central information source for the feminist movement makes our self-assured interpretations somewhat presumptuous: A diffuse movement simply does not lend itself to facile definitions. It's difficult to begin to explain "The women's movement is . . ." and hope to complete the explanation comprehensively. Yet given the healthy chance that this movement *does* constitute the most significant and far-reaching reform attempt that our age is to see, attempts both to understand and to interpret are not misplaced.

Currents of feminist thought, and trends of movement ideology, may be perceived perhaps through the simplest of all approaches—using a composite of typical conversations, situations, events, and happenings to arrive at a central reality *from* individual occasions: an impressionistic, inductive approach.

The women's movement from this standpoint is:

    —A gathering of elegantly attired women, many accompanied by men, in an upper East Side New York penthouse, balancing cocktail glasses delicately as they listen to a U.N. official discuss an International Women's Year Arts Festival, applauding as a noted gallery owner pledges "priority for exhibitions by women artists during International Women's Year."

—A gathering of carelessly dressed women sitting with paper coffee cups in a vacant room on lower La Cienega Boulevard in Los Angeles, hearing a cultural anthropologist explain away "male chauvinist nonprimate studies" which once had seemed to imply biologically based differences of temperament and levels of aggression between the sexes. (There are cheers for a photo of female monkeys putting to rout a dominant male who had been monopolizing a mushroom bed.)

—The brazen, insightful, nutty media "zap" conducted by Flo Kennedy's masked demonstrators outside the Pierre Hotel on Halloween 1974, protesting Channel 13's employment policies—or the one staged by Anita Murray to protest abortion restrictions, with a dozen or more feminists cannily costumed as saints—or the "invasion" of NBC by Lesbian Feminist Liberation forces who had pretended to tour a popular quiz show, then made their way through unused stairwells to the executive office floor, to dramatically present their demand that a program stereotyping lesbians as systematic murderers of helpless senior citizens be withdrawn from the program schedule.

The women's movement is also the practical, service-oriented discussions, in every major city, which help older women face aging, divorced women find jobs, and housewives begin CR groups.

It is the standing-room-only conference on *Fly Me*, sponsored by Stewardesses for Women's Rights, to "declare war on all airlines who engage in sexploitation," at which a stewardess declares, "I'm not a sex object or a servant. I'm someone who is capable of opening the door of a 747 in the dark, upside down, and in the water."

It is the total vigilance of "Joyce's team," a group of twenty women who, day in, week out, sit before their television sets, notebooks in hand, to record discriminatory images of women . . . gathering ammunition for future license challenges and other protests.

It is Karen DeCrow leading two hundred women delegates to NOW's counter-convention in a parade along the Atlantic City boardwalk on the day of the Miss America pageant; and a young woman in a town called Sapulpa, Oklahoma, hesitating at the drugstore magazine rack as she begins to reach for *Redbook*, then thinks that this month, just for a change, she'll buy a copy of *Ms.* instead.

The women's movement is a soft-spoken, self-proclaimed feminist pleading with members of her bridge club (in a Montana town so remote it's only touched by a narrow-gauge railroad track, where the Chicago *Tribune* arrives three days late) to understand that asking her husband to help with the housework *hasn't harmed* her marriage. She draws a careful distinction between "helping" and "doing his share," but she's only after the former because she doesn't believe in "going too far, too fast."

And it's also three lesbian separatists in a carefree rap at Mother Courage restaurant on a summer New York evening, recalling the "brutish" techniques their male partners used to use to achieve maximum penetration during intercourse, talking not with exaggerated salaciousness or scorn but with the sincere gratitude of those who've left an awful past behind. "The worst kind of guy will grab your ankles and then force your knees back so he can operate better—Christ, you feel like a wheelbarrow—call it the

Miami Fuck, a guy from Miami did it to me first. . . .'
They stare at the heterosexual couple two tables away
whose appearance started their conversation. They do not
lower their voices as they talk.

The women's movement comes at us in much this way:
as a series of varied, sometimes confusing, and sometimes
conflicting images. And as one attempts to sort out the
impressions, the suspicion grows that *what our society is
facing right now is not one women's movement, but two.*

Feminists themselves separate the movement into two
philosophical branches, *feminism* and *radical feminism*,
each with its own architecture for change. Feminism is the
movement's mainstream (begun by Betty Friedan and continued by the organization she founded, the National Organization for Women); radical feminism is that aggregate
of tributaries sometimes regarded as troublesome by
Friedan and other moderates.

Feminism is basically an *assimilation* model that accepts the present structure of society as stable and desirable,
and urges women to win their rightful place within that
system, accepting the goals and values of the dominant
group as their own; radical feminism is a *departure* model
that rejects the present structure of society and seeks instead a new breed of men and women and a new vision of
the future.*

"Radical feminism," explains Bonnie Kreps in her
essay of that title, "is called 'radical' because it is struggling
to bring about really fundamental changes in our society.
We, in this segment of the movement, do not believe that
the oppression of women will be ended by giving them a

*Feminism is establishment-oriented even in language and tactics; rad-
ical feminism models itself on national and ethnic revolutionary movements. For example, feminists set up organizations (notably, NOW)
that operate by *committees* and *task forces*; radical feminists term their
working units *cadres*.

bigger piece of the pie, as Betty Friedan would have it. We believe that the pie itself is rotten."[1]

Thus, radical feminist Ti-Grace Atkinson, originally a friend of Friedan and president of NOW, explained her resignation from that office by saying, "I realize that by holding this office I am participating in oppression itself. You cannot destroy oppression by filling the position of the oppressor."

Feminists and radical feminists hold one principle in common. Central to both philosophies is the goal of *equality* for women, the enjoyment of the same independence with which men have traditionally been favored by all societies. In this, of course, feminists are following history. In 1792 Mary Wollstonecraft wrote, "Independence I have long considered to be life's grand blessing," and feminists from Harriet Martineau to Ti-Grace Atkinson have echoed her. Notably, Simone de Beauvoir wrote, in *The Second Sex*,

> Woman has always been man's dependent, if not his slave; the two sexes have never shared the world in equality. And even today woman is heavily handicapped, though her situation is beginning to change. Almost nowhere is her legal status the same as man's, and frequently it is much to her disadvantage. Even when her rights are legally recognized in the abstract, long-standing custom prevents their full expression in the mores. In the economic sphere men and women can be almost said to be two castes; other things being equal, the former hold the better jobs, get higher wages, and have more opportunity for success than their new competitors. In industry and politics men have a great many more positions and they monopolize the most important posts. In addition to all this, they enjoy a traditional prestige that the education of children tends in every way to support, for the present enshrines the past. . . .[2]

Today both feminists and radical feminists are determined that the present shall *un*enshrine the past. To De Beauvoir's overview of ways in which women are made to depend on men—legal, economic, and political—this decade's generation of feminists has added new considerations, of psychological and sexual repression. Thus a broader concept of "equality" emerges.

It all began, this time around, in 1963, with Friedan: It began with her recognition that modern women were living a lie. Considered to be "the envy of women all over the world—freed by science and labor-saving appliances from the drudgery, the dangers of childbirth and the illnesses of her grandmother; healthy, educated, concerned only about her husband, her children, her home, the possessor of "true feminine fulfillment,' "[3] these women were in fact *not happy.*

These women, Friedan perceived, who sat over coffee at one another's houses in the early 1960s, were sleeping too much, drinking immoderately, dallying desperately with ceramics, garden clubs, and child-raising theories, and were beginning to awaken from a false contentment that society had drugged them into accepting. They were beginning to realize that something inside them gnawed and gnawed, and would not go away.

They complained eventually, first to one another, then in public, of "the problem that had no name"—though elements of it were loveless marriages, unused talents, a sense of purposelessness which seemed to permeate their lives. Ceramics did not help—nor, ultimately, did Valium, therapy, another child, a weekend home, a second station wagon. Was their discontent irrational, or was something really wrong?

Something *was* wrong, they were told by Ms. Friedan

and others. They needed equality, not domination; direct experience, not vicarious living through husband and children; productivity and stimulation in the real world of work, not the material comforts of a womblike suburban duplex; achievement in meaningful careers, not more and better garden clubs.

Most of all they needed emancipation from the feminine mystique, from a concept of themselves as secondary beings, passive consumers, decorative sex objects.

Thus spake Friedan, and rather sensibly.

To reread her book now, to recall the inspiring words about the achievement of completeness as a human being *and* as a woman, is to realize with some astonishment how far the movement has come from the vision of the author of *The Feminine Mystique.*

The goal was of course full personhood. But the methods were intended neither to redefine woman's nature nor to disrupt traditionally established relationships between men and women. The means to liberation, Friedan stresses, was simply, "creative work of her own . . . a job that she can take seriously as part of a life plan, work in which she can grow as part of society." Here's how simply this could be achieved, as Friedan wrote,

> One woman I interviewed had involved herself in an endless whirl of worthwhile community activities. But they led in no direction for her own future, nor did they truly utilize her intelligence. Indeed, her intelligence seemed to deteriorate: she suffered the problem that has no name with increasing severity until she took the first step toward a serious commitment. Today, she is a "master teacher," a serene wife and mother.[4]

Taken out of context, that example seems perhaps *too* simple, too calculatedly inspirational. Still I don't disbelieve it, and have in fact known many variations on it. There's an implication not to be missed: the implication that not only did this woman's job as a teacher give her "creative work of her own" but also allowed her to be a *better*—more "serene"—wife and mother. Her domestic and productive roles complemented one another.

Nowhere, at any time, did Friedan speak of leaving one's home, rejecting men, or defining love as a tool or technique of oppression.

In fact, "When a few runaway mothers published articles on their experiences, word was passed down that den mother Friedan had snapped, 'That was never what we intended!' "[5]

What Friedan seemed to be after was instead the *integration* of love and work, the fuller potential for developing love and caring, enhanced by the increased self-worth a woman might expect to find through work. Her closing words in fact were,

> Who knows what women can be when they are finally free to become themselves? Who knows what woman's intelligence will contribute when it can be nourished without denying love? Who knows of the possibilities of love when men and women share not only children, home, and garden, not only the fulfillment of their biological roles, but the responsibilities and passions of the work that creates the human future and the full human knowledge of who they are. . . .[6]

One wonders what might have happened if that message had remained central to the movement: if the generation of women to whom Friedan wrote had sought to follow her prescription of sharing, had sought to *add* to the established ideal of "home . . . biological roles" while *still retaining* these things as ideals of worth. A significant de-

gree of aggressive political action could still have been predicted (there were and are barriers to women becoming
"master teachers," let alone modestly successful executives
or lawyers or whatever), but it might have stopped far short
of denouncing love as a male chauvinist plot.

But the idea of liberation that Friedan reintroduced in
1963, the spark of dormant feminism she rekindled, quickly
established a life of its own; it spread like electricity, leapt
like flame, and no one—not even Friedan—was able to
control it. And somehow, within a very few years, the idea
that the feminine mystique was damaging transformed itself into the notion that feminity itself in all its facets was
undesirable.

For example, in rejection of the beauty ideal, Lisa
Hobbs wrote,

> Our bodies are no longer objects to be corseted and
> spread with pastes or to be distorted in shape and texture
> to build a false image. . . . We are beginning to see our
> bodies in their most natural, spontaneous forms.
> Younger women are refusing to fetter their breasts with
> brassieres, and butter their faces with makeup; older
> women are dressing more casually, more comfortably.
> They are beginning to let their graying hair stay
> gray . . . to face the world the way they really are.[7]*

Femininity was seen by radical feminists as an aggregate
of characteristics, both outer and internalized, ideals of
both physical allure and emotional conciliation, cultivated
through the centuries to please men. And men were not
worthy of all that effort. ("Pandering to the male ego is

---

*There were a few curious examples of what might be called backslid-
ing, however. In *The Female Eunuch*, Germaine Greer declared, "I'm
sick of peering at the world through false eyelashes"; yet in the cover
photograph of that book, as in most of her publicity appearances, she is
clearly wearing extremely heavy false eyelashes.

finished!") Men were, in fact, defined according to the new radical feminists as The Enemy.

Ti-Grace Atkinson asked,

> If "society" is the enemy, what could that mean? If women are being oppressed, there's only one group left over to be doing the oppressing: men. Then why call them "society"? Should "society" mean the institutions that oppress women? But institutions must be maintained, and the same question arises: by whom? The answer to "Who is the enemy?" is so obvious that the interesting issue quickly becomes "Why has it been avoided?" The master might tolerate many reforms in slavery but none that would threaten his essential role as master. Women have known this, and since "men" and "society" are in effect synonymous, they have feared confronting him.[8]

No more.

"Oppressors: The curse of women is on you," warned an organization called WITCH (Women's International Terrorist Conspiracy from Hell), fancifully replacing Virginia Woolf's yearning for a room of one's own with calls for a broom of one's own, hexing establishment strongholds with surrealistic "zaps" designed to draw media attention, brewing such thought-provoking slogans as "Up Against the Wall Street."

With somewhat less good humor, Valerie Solanis announced the formation of SCUM, the Society for Cutting Up Men. She spoke of the desirability of "destroying the male sex" and wrote, "The male is a biological accident, an incomplete female, a walking abortion, aborted at the gene state"*; wrote, "SCUM will couple-bust, barge into mixed

---

*It is now believed that the human fetus is originally physically female, until the operation of androgen at a certain stage of gestation causes those fetuses with Y chromosomes to develop into males.

(male-female) couples, wherever they are, and bust them up"; wrote, simply, "SCUM will kill all men who are not in the Men's Auxiliary of SCUM."[9]

Joreen, a Chicago radical feminist, proclaimed in "Bitch Manifesto" that "Bitches are aggressive, assertive, domineering, overbearing, strong-minded, spiteful, hostile, direct, blunt, candid, obnoxious, thick-skinned, hard-headed, vicious, dogmatic, competent, competitive, pushy, loud-mouthed, independent, stubborn, demanding, manipulative, egoistic, driven, achieving, overwhelming, threatening, scary, ambitious, tough, brassy, masculine, boisterous, and turbulent," and that "A woman should be proud to declare she is a bitch, because bitch is beautiful."[10]

It should have been obvious that the feminist pursuit of equality was taking off in some funny directions. If Hobbs's advice to toss out the lipstick and undergarments ("and face the world the way we really are") didn't suffice to indicate danger, Joreen's "Bitch Manifesto" should have. The clear and apparent danger was that equality of opportunity and treatment had become confused with *identicality*—with a wholesale adoption of the motive patterns, lifestyles, virtues *and vices* of men. Suddenly, in 1970, everybody wanted to be equal, but almost nobody asked *"Equal to what?"* (Nobody asked Joreen what was so "beautiful" about being "tough, brassy, masculine, egoistic, and driven.") Curious and ironic as it might seem, some feminists apparently believed that equality would be attained when they had the power to treat others as badly as they had perceived themselves to have been treated: *these feminists were emulating the very beings they were defining as "enemy."* The emancipation of women now augured male-emulation—and man-hating.

With stunning simplicity, Pamela Kearon defended the concept of man-hating in somewhat this way: Hatred is an observable human fact. Women are human. Thus they will hate someone. It makes more sense to hate with reason than at random. And it's men who are the bastards; it's men who oppress women. So it's logical for women to hate men.

Even Hobbs (regarded as a moderate radical on the West Coast) admitted, "It would be false to deny that the element which will ultimately hold both conservatives and radicals together in some loose form of alliance is an antagonism toward the male."

Of course, there was one hang-up. One can only hate what one no longer needs, since something needed must, from a functional standpoint be regarded with an attitude of gratitude or protectiveness. Thus there remained the not-insignificant matter of sex, for which men and women supposedly needed each other, and thus (on their half of that equation) for which women needed men. To circumvent this, the radical feminist movement produced a classic paper by Anne Koedt called "The Myth of the Vaginal Orgasm," to establish that female sexual satisfaction did not depend on male penetration. "If genital tensions persist, masturbate," was a widely quoted dictum emanating from Dana Densmore's radical feminist circle in Boston; and Washington, D.C.'s Rita Mae Brown added several colorful phrases to radical feminist rhetoric, such as an essay bidding farewell to the "Age of Spermatic Oppression."

It was popular to dismiss Solanis and Brown as radical fringe, media novelties, their verbal terrorism of no consequence. Sometimes it was indeed meaningless (SCUM and BITCH never had any reality as organizations); at other times, though, small threads of theory, publication, or personal acquaintance held the fringe to the fabric of radical feminism.

No one, for example would take Solanis's actual words seriously; but Solanis was a friend of Ti-Grace Atkinson and Atkinson was a force to be dealt with; and at the core of what Joreen and WITCH held in common with more responsible radical theorists was the aim, not of restructuring relations between the sexes, but of obviating the need for intersex relationships at all.

Probably the most deeply reasoned, widely read, and internally influential theorists of radical feminism were Ti-Grace Atkinson and Shulamith Firestone. Their vision of the future differed considerably from Friedan's.

Friedan merely wanted women to have access to birth control and abortion. Firestone wanted "the freeing of women from the tyranny of their reproductive biology," and from childbearing altogether. The day-care centers Friedan called for, Firestone termed "a timid if not entirely worthless transition. We need *radical* change . . . the potential of modern embryology, artificial reproduction.

"Radical goals must be kept in sight at all times," Firestone stressed. "Day-care centers buy women off. They ease the immediate pressure without asking why that pressure is on *women*."

This brought up the issue of family, for the family had indeed been structured so that women took care of children; and therefore if women wanted out, it was up to the women to find their own alternatives. Friedan did not call for an end to family structure in order to deal with this problem; Firestone did. Firestone saw that freeing women from their biology would also free them from the social unit which had been organized around biological reproduction —*i.e.*, the family.

Ti-Grace Atkinson also favored abolition of the family, the establishment of extrauterine reproduction, and identification of men as the enemy. She postulated that "A woman can unite with a man only as long as she is a *woman* (*i.e.*, subordinate) but not longer." And women should end this state of subordination and dependency as soon as possible, since "The price of clinging to the enemy is your life."

It would be a mistake to think that a majority of women bought the messages of either feminism or radical feminism, and one can almost choose one's evidential indices at will (*The Total Woman* sold over 350,000 copies, Kate Millett's *Flying* only 15,000); but for those who did, what happened? Sometimes rejection of the traditional female role worked for women, often it didn't. Sometimes women, wanting something *more*, found after the transition that they had something *other*, and had lost in the process whatever flawed comforts family life promised, or had held for them before.

And, for many who bought the message, the bills are arriving. There seems to be a lot of bitterness in the air, a lot of discontent. The women's liberation movement has directly (or much more often, indirectly) raised women's expectations of what constitutes a full and rich, good and productive and independent life. In pursuit of that goal, marriages and other intimate arrangements have been abandoned. (If this was not intended, it is nonetheless happening—some version of it even happened to Friedan.)

Perhaps it's obvious that the first generation of emancipated women (like the first generation of freed slaves) resents former oppressors or oppressive domestic arrangements, finds friendship and interaction with the power class difficult. It's somewhat more surprising to find former oppressions yearned-for.

Yet sometimes they are. One year after a leading feminist proposed "*resistance* . . . against the concrete conditions of women's oppression . . . when it begins to get dark, instead of cooking dinner or making love, we will assemble, and we will carry candles symbolic of that flame of the passionate journey down through history . . . our revolution will be a fact!"[11] this same feminist wrote an article for *McCall's*, speaking somewhat lyrically of cooking dinner and making love in an article entitled "We Don't Have to Be *That* Independent."[12]

And several years after Anne Koedt and others exploded the myth of any need for heterosexual intercourse, a radical feminist in the pages of *Ms.* magazine proclaimed, "I want to get laid." Perhaps some of the perceived oppressions weren't oppressions after all, or at least not to all women.

Questions being quietly raised by women touched by the movement deserve close scrutiny now, while the feminist wave is still crescent, and changes in direction and philosophy are possible. Have we perhaps discarded tenderness, affection, and mutually supportive relationships in favor of a mere obsession with orgasm? Is the search for sex and status creating not liberated women but counterfeit men? Have women escaped from the prison of the feminine mystique only to find new confinement within the *masculine* mystique? Have we begun to abandon values that may be our only hope for the future?

Movements are always built around concepts—in this case concepts such as dependence, exploitation, oppression of women. But such concepts are mere airy matter, for all their weighty sound; and feminism is, at heart, not the messages and concepts but the *women themselves* who consider the concepts, accept the theories, and change their lives as a result. Thus the women's movement is less about the neurotic nature of female passivity, the exploitative nature of power and powerlessness, and the oppression by males of females, than it is about such women as Madeline and Sammie, Lila and Rona and Sonia—and their efforts to establish personal power over their own lives, and find fulfillment in new and individual ways: Madeline through sexual expression, Lila and Sammie through devotion to the movement itself, Rona through other women —and Sonia, who achieved what almost anyone would define as emotional liberation, but found it didn't last.

Central, somehow, to all their stories is the matter of dependence. They all attempted certainly to be independent, but only one, I think, succeeded. The rest were left as tragically dependent as before: They only changed the things on which they leaned.

It's dependence, too, around which all the identifiable issues of the movement seem to orbit, the central concept to which all other theories and subissues attach themselves, as moss to rock. Whether one talks of divorce law or day care, the ERA, the liberated orgasm, media image, or the need for female training in the martial arts, it's *women's dependence on a male-dominated system* that is the evil to be rooted out, the oppressive weight to be cast off, the trap from which women need to be freed.

Just how well is the process going?

Madeline:

"Nobody Gave Me A Medal"

Some take a lover, some take drams or prayers,
Some mind their household, other dissipation,
Some run away, and but exchange their cares,
Losing the advantage of a virtuous station. . . .

Somehow, in seeking to explain her life, Madeline began with the sixth grade. "Isn't there a kind of girl who is always the star of the sixth grade? Who hands homework in on time, is never absent, always gets A's, always has her essays read aloud, always knows how to spell *benefited*, can explain why the horse died in "The Red Pony," and remembers there are forty-six chromosomes in a cell . . . and whose papers always have neat margins?

"That was me," said Madeline to a counselor in the spring of 1973.

"Not that I wasn't good in earlier grades, too. But I was only bright, not exceptional, because you see lots of girls are bright students in the early grades! But most of these 'bright' girls begin to drop out intellectually when dating becomes crucial, when they learn the rules of the game, and sense that if they seem too brainy they won't be asked out.

"The year that happened for my crowd was the year we were in sixth grade. My girlfriends who'd formerly competed with me for the most A's suddenly put on the brakes—began to 'compete' in a way that was a lot more shrewd, a lot less clear-cut. They wanted to do well—that was still satisfying to them—but they didn't want to do too well or it would interfere with their new social goals. If they lost control and did their best in classes and got all *A*'s just from habit, you always knew it because they refused to show you their report cards.

"Maybe that doesn't happen anymore, but that's the way it was in Hammond, Indiana, when I was in the sixth grade. I simply held out longer than the other girls. That's why the sixth grade was so memorable to me: I was the only bright girl in that class, or so it seemed. That was the year I even won the Williams Medal, the all-school medal for spelling, won out even over all the seventh and eighth graders. . . .

"I couldn't hold out beyond my sophomore year, though. A week before the homecoming game, I was the only girl in my crowd who hadn't been asked to the game . . . and I had a library date with a dull guy on the same day we were to get back our unit papers on Fitzgerald. To my dismay, I got an *A* plus, and the teacher had written 'Most original!' beside one of my paragraphs which linked the theme of pursuit of the ineffable and unobtainable Daisy to the poem which began the book and which, I suggested, might have been inspired by Keats's 'Ode on a Grecian Urn.' Keeping my mouth shut about my grade, I asked around and found that the boy who was my date that night had gotten a *B* plus.

"A girl friend said to me, 'Don't worry about the game. Maybe tonight you'll get asked to it. In fact, I'm sure you will. You're much too pretty to end up like Angie.' "

"*Angie*. Angie was a senior and she was probably going to be salutatorian but she had never had a date! I seemed to look ahead and see nothing but a tunnel, a trap, getting narrower and darker as my case became more and more hopeless, like Angie's, until no boy could ever ask me out just because no other boy ever had.

"Unless, of course, I acted somehow. . . . 'Pretend you need help with your next paper or something,' my girl friend advised helpfully, 'Guys like that.'

"Taking no chances, I planned to do even more. . . .

"Right after school, I begged my teacher to change my grade, telling her I'd prefer not to be given fair credit for my work if it meant being typecast as an intellectual freak, and I feared that that was exactly what was happening. She refused, lecturing me about being true to my talents and not selling out. Rather a nice lecture, but of course I didn't absorb a word of it, already planning a different strategy. I rushed to buy some ink eradicator and a red grading pen: then I went home, shut the bedroom door, and with heart pounding changed the *A* on my paper to a *B* and the *plus* to a *minus*, and then—this was most difficult—obliterated the *most* of the '*most original*' and finally, practicing on a separate sheet of paper so that my handwriting would match the teacher's, changed her comment to '*Not* original *enough.*'

"I was sweating and shaking so much after that—but happy. I felt so much in control, felt some kind of intuition, some predictive intuition that told me that if I showed my altered paper to my date and pretended to be depressed about the *B* minus I'd have a date for the game. And it happened that way, so smoothly that I almost felt contempt for him for his predictable, unoriginal response. He was almost like a pawn, I thought. It didn't occur to me that I was, too. Not then, not yet.

"I began to date, to be popular. Repressing my mind became just another intellectual game at which I could be proficient. That wasn't difficult. But there was something else I was repressing, too—not only my mind, but my body. In Hammond, Indiana, at that time, not only were 'nice girls' not smart, they were not sexual. And though that area of repression was a little more confusing at first, I figured it out as well. The thing to do was tease until you got a guy aroused, then act shy and reticent, as though surprised at what you'd done . . . and always murmur, 'But we shouldn't,' no matter how much you wanted to scream, 'Oh yes, let's.'

"It's what we all did; I simply did it with more convincing subtlety and near-sincerity than others. I was simply better at it than a lot of girls, therefore more popular.

"I began to set definite goals for myself in terms of what boy I wanted to interest, and how I could best do this. The football quarterback, the yearbook editor, the debating captain. If anybody ever writes about the social machinery of the adolescent fifties, they should devote a chapter to me as the perfect cog. I allowed intercourse with my steady after the senior prom and married him three weeks after high school graduation. He was, of course, the football quarterback—he was also the son of Hammond, Indiana's leading physician, and headed for a lucrative career as a medical equipment salesman, since he wasn't quite gifted enough to follow in his daddy's footsteps as an M.D.

"It had all worked, you see. I had cultivated myself as carefully as a rare flower, weeded out all the 'incorrect' ideas that threatened to sprout from time to time, pruned back my self and my thoughts and ultimately bloomed in a way that pleased everyone around me. I have to admit that I was pleased, too. Pretty smug, in fact. In spite of myself, I have to think back on how comfortable life was. . . .

"Our first apartment was the top floor of a small Tudor

house in Hammond, with space where I could have a garden out back. I cooked, decorated the apartment with superb skill, read novels, learned ceramics, and developed a real passion for my garden. . . .

"Oh, and I entertained, too. And I didn't resent it, not at the time. I somehow felt a real pride at creating gracious evenings, in helping to advance Jerry's career while still having my own pattern of life during the day, being free to do whatever my impulses directed. It was a little more difficult after the baby came—perhaps substantially more difficult—but still my schedule was basically my own; I didn't *have* to have the baby at the playground at 10 A.M. when all the other mothers promptly brought their children there. I believe I was a happy woman, content as a housewife and mother.

"There was, of course, an underlying falsity to it, and I'd never have been able to delude myself for those eight years of marriage without almost daily brainwashing from the women's magazines I used to read. . . .

"Oh, I read those magazines constantly! For almost an hour at some time during every day, I'd sit clipping casserole recipes or coupons for new cleaning products or practically memorizing some inspirational 'Happy Housewife' article.

"I was doing everything correctly, still. My home always looked precisely arranged, neat and attractive enough to be a magazine feature, but people around me— neighbors, relatives, and Jerry—seemed to take this homemaking excellence more and more for granted. They didn't realize there was a lot of effort involved to create this constantly perfect picture, to keep some stray toy or overflowing ashtray or dirty coffee cup from throwing the picture out of focus. I guess there came a stirring in me that caused me to want some recognition for the fact that *my* house (unlike the neighbors') was never disorganized, always had fresh flowers, interesting music, and the latest books, nice aromas from coffee or baking . . . that *my* house was peopled with a usually happy child and an always attractive *me*!

"Mine, I would say, was an *A* plus house. My neighbor's houses, by contrast, seemed to rate at most a *B* minus. I remember remarking to Jerry once that somebody should give me a Good Housekeeping Seal of Approval.

"But this wasn't the sixth grade anymore.

"Nobody came to the door to give me a medal and say, 'Congratulations: you're doing a fine job, you're the best housewife and most sensitive mother and most intelligent consumer in Hammond, Indiana, and on behalf of Society I want you to know that we are all grateful.'

"Nobody gave me a medal. Nobody gave me a merit raise or a testimonial dinner or a 'Most Congenial' award or a sales bonus or a letter of commendation.

"Why bother?, I began to wonder. But I couldn't stop trying. When I tried to talk these feelings over with Jerry, he suggested I enter some of my plants in garden shows. But a few blue ribbons for the greenhouse violets didn't help.

"I bought Betty Friedan's book but couldn't get into it; nevertheless, I began to think about getting a job. Just thought about it, though. Then Germaine Greer's book came out. *That* had a real impact on me. Everything she wrote made sense.

"It tore the whole facade away. I really learned what had happened to me in my sophomore year. Why did it take a dozen years and a woman from another country to make me see my history so clearly—to make me see that

powerful sex-role stereotypes had acted like a current to
sweep me from the direction of intellectual development I
should have followed, taking me to that terrible moment in
my sophomore year when I sat down with ink eradicator
and *eradicated all I could have been.* Germaine Greer described my situation: 'If intellect impedes feminization, intellect must go.' Ah, that's the way it was. . . .

   "But there was more. Remember that in high school I
had repressed not only my intellect, but my sexuality. I
wanted to shout, with Greer, 'Yes, women *do* have sexual
desire . . . we *must* reinstate our libido to its rightful function.' I wondered what sort of fuller, richer woman I would
have become.had I been able to read Germaine Greer's
book during my sophomore year. I envied all the sophomore high-school girls who could read the book then. One
day, I thought, perhaps I could help bring the thoughts of
feminists such as Germaine Greer to high school
girls. . . ."

   But personal action came first. Taking Greer's scorn
for female sexual passivity to heart, Madeline that night
announced to her husband that she considered herself to be
a sexual castrate, who had never had the will or courage to
seek real sexual enjoyment . . . so perhaps it's no wonder
she had never had it, but she'd like to change the situation
now, and here is what the facts were. First, her sex life with
him was not satisfying to her, had never been. She brought
up a deeply submerged memory to the surface of her mind:
That first time he had penetrated her, after all their weeks
of fumbling, hotly touching one another but outside the
clothing only, of course (that was what the rules were); after
all those stirring, rousing episodes of what he oh-so-very-
crudely called dry humping (being deliberately crude as
part of an effort to win Madeline to the beauty of 'the real

thing') . . . did he remember that first time, when he had seemed so moved, so grateful? "Do you remember afterwards, Jerry, when you said, 'Thank you Madeline, oh thank you'?" (Burying his face in her shoulder. Yes, he remembered.) "You know I was so surprised at your saying that. I had an impulse to say to you politely, 'Oh you're welcome, Jerry, it was nothing.'" Because that is what she'd felt—nothing, or nearly nothing. And she'd expected so much— "I had expected to feel more, I kept expecting to feel more, and never have. Can you understand that, Jerry?"

She talked on. She seldom achieved orgasm, she explained. Further, she'd like to question the unspoken agreement that had always characterized their sex relations, according to which he and only he initiated a sex act. She had always done her best to accommodate him: so wasn't it only right that her sexual nature be acknowledged, some reciprocity instituted? Couldn't he pay attention to her needs, as she had always done to his? She believes she recalls quoting Greer to the effect that she was not merely asking for mechanistic improvement, though of course that was involved: but further she had a right "not just to orgasm, but to ecstasy."

"Surely there has to be more to sex than what you and I have had," she thinks she remembers saying.

"Surely there has to be more. . . ."

The resilience of the human spirit in the face of natural disaster, historic adversity, and personal loss and pain tests, at times, the boundaries of credibility: One thinks humbly of those thousands of anonymous men and women whose parents and whose children die, whose crops are lost to drought, homes destroyed by flood or fire, or livelihood and personhood made meaningless by changing times. . . .

Yet while great disasters may be weathered because their very magnitude mobilizes the total resources of the personality, sometimes *small* disasters catch by surprise, touch some nerve or frailty within us, and paralyze. Can we not all remember some casual or offhand remark, made cruel by manner or ill-timing, which we received or gave, which altered us for years? If, according to one poet, in times of trauma, "there is some word, some simple word, which tells us nothing and yet calms us," then conversely in times of relative well-being there can be an insult which ought not to affect us profoundly—and which destroys.

"Well, you should have said something sooner," said Madeline's husband casually, and went to pour himself an unaccustomed Scotch.

"Did you really mean that—what you said the other night?" he asked her on succeeding evenings. "Yes, I did," she said at first, uncompromising; then, stricken with fear or guilt, began to change her answer to, "No, I didn't . . ." "No, all I meant was that . . ." and then to "No, of course not, I was so silly; come over to the sofa and let's have a drink and talk; do you like the way I look tonight?"

Her husband over the ensuing months remained solicitous and kindly—and impotent.

The two considered going to the Masters and Johnson clinic in St. Louis, hesitated after hearing that someone from Jerry's company had gone to work there, fearful that the neighbors (or Jerry's father) would find out. Madeline joined a CR group but remained silent or vague when sexuality in marriage was discussed: no help to be found there.

Finally, Jerry had an inspiration: He would take Madeline on a trip to South America, to search in the highlands for orchids for her greenhouse; she'd been yearning after orchids. Surely, away from home, in a romantic setting, the unfamiliar pleasures of a foreign place, away from that living room dominated by the severe green sofa where she'd sat when she told him that . . . Who could tell? They might even move to a new house when they returned; surely things would somehow be all right again.

The inspiration didn't work: perhaps it was the food, the wine, the air, the altitude, the water; or perhaps just the realization that this impulsive journey had, after all, been some nebulous hope or fantasy.

How unrealistic, how incredibly unrealistic, to expect a mere change of setting to mend broken patterns of stimulus and response, to reconstruct the frayed fabric of male pride, to alter visceral responses which had, despite the best conscious intentions, hardened into resolutions. How unrealistic, yet how typically so—entire segments of the travel-and-leisure economy must be built on such hopes as Jerry and Madeline had nourished. As it was, however, Jerry spent his days with Scotch and Lomatil, while Madeline scoured the hillsides with a guide in search of the tulip orchids, in search of *Anguloa* and the even rarer *Anguloa uniflora*. . . .

On the last leg of the complicated flight schedule taking them back to Indiana, they began to speak. Jerry announced that he rather thought he would go into counseling, and they'd "see what happened." In the meantime, he suggested, Madeline might want to consider taking a lover, "as long as it could be done discreetly." Compounding previous errors of tactlessness, she said, "I'm sorry, but I couldn't wait for your permission to do that: I already have."

She made an effort to atone for that after their arrival

home that evening. "You've been so good to me in so many ways," she said to him. "And in so many ways I've been childish, blurting out my own demands and needs. Do you think we could forget what I said on the plane, Jerry? Do you think we could just forget that conversation we had months ago, about that silly Greer book? We'll pretend it never happened, or we'll have a *different* talk about it, a more mature and fair talk. You're such a strong, good-looking man, Jerry. And you used to think I was attractive—do you still? Listen, there's no reason we can't make it work together, honey—don't you think that we could really try?" She was following her own intuitions now, no book for guideline.

"I think, Jerry . . . I think the key is spontaneity. We have to be more spontaneous with each other, the way we sometimes were before Timmy was born, and we can build that spontaneity again, and build *on* it. . . ." She closed her eyes. "Oh, Jerry, I want to try everything, *just everything*, do you understand that? But only if you want to as well. . . ."

She spoke on and on, her words punctuated now and then by Jerry nodding absently, or shaking his head, or making some small comment, or pouring himself another drink. Madeline took her sandals off as she spoke, drew both legs up on the sofa, brushed her hair back with her hand, continued talking. . . .

"I really think that you're a terrific guy, Jerry," she said about 10:30, and their eyes met, and as she was formulating just the right thing to say next—suggestive but undemanding—Timmy woke up, calling for her from his bedroom; and, needing reassurance that his mother was home again, he fussed for about twenty minutes before going back to sleep in Madeline's arms. And by the time

Madeline put out Timmy's light and went hastily to their own bedroom, hers and Jerry's, the room was dark and Jerry was pretending sleep with loud, false snores. She undressed, slipped between the sheets and touched his shoulder, but he did not respond. And, in the morning, and in the coming weeks, husband and wife began in their own minds the process of separation. Jerry asked his company for more out-of-town sales trips. Madeline, for her part, brushed up on her typing, saw a job counselor, became annoyed that the lack of a day-care center near her might prevent her from taking a job, joined a local feminist group to agitate for community child-care facilities, and joined another CR group.

Privately, she continued to be somewhat obsessed with the subject of her own sexuality, feeling she had never been fully appreciated as a woman. She had had only predictable, "permissible" intercourse, safe but unexciting, within her marriage; and a few afternoon interludes with a nervous lover who parked his car five blocks away, then ten, then *more*, and finally gave up coming over altogether for fear of discovery. Besides, she estimated that even with this lover she had had only light orgasms (three to five contractions, as she recalled). Surely there was more, worlds more.

She lacked the candor to discuss sex in her new CR group; so she, like Jerry, found a private counselor, to whom she told the preceding story.

And she read. Eclectically. From *Sex in Human Loving* to *Human Sexual Response* to *Rubyfruit Jungle* and *Lesbian Nation* and *Sexual Politics* and *The Erotic Life of the American Wife*. She took notes. Perhaps the time would come when she could discuss what she was reading with Jerry, perhaps not. In any case, she would have the notes.

In the spring of 1973 a brochure reached the Hammond Women's Center describing the Sexuality Conference sponsored by NOW in New York, "to define, explore, and celebrate our own sexuality." Madeline determined to attend that conference. Four women planned to drive East together, but two changed their minds; so Madeline and another woman, Lorna, would leave on Thursday morning, in a 1969 Ford station wagon, for the twenty-hour drive. Madeline, waiting for Lorna in the semidark and total silence of the beautifully decorated apartment that nobody had ever given her a medal for, wrote careful instructions to her husband and to the housekeeper who would arrive for the weekend. The plants should be shielded from too much direct sunlight, Timmy must have juice at 10 A.M. and milk and cookies in the afternoon. . . . Tiptoeing into the bedroom, she left Jerry's envelope on the bedside table. He did not awake, or seemed not to.

Madeline and Lorna were among the first of over one thousand women (and some men) to register for the conference at P.S. 99 on Saturday, June 13. For validation of her own distress, the opening event of the conference was all, or more, than Madeline could have hoped for. Woman after woman took the microphone to describe how she had escaped from past frustrations of orgasmic incompleteness; they told of the sometimes arduous struggles with their minds and bodies which had finally brought them to "peaks of erotic pleasure."

One woman (*who could be me*, thought Madeline) told of reading Millett and Greer and then confronting her husband with her own feelings of frustration. "He didn't seem to care," the woman moaned. "Can you believe it? He wouldn't even talk about it, turned me off completely. How I longed to have some good contact with him! I wanted to share with him the studies of clitoral response, those fantastic studies about multiple orgasms, wanted to ask him if he wouldn't think it a trip to turn me on more than he ever had. . . ." And then she said the words that brought cheers and applause: "But he wasn't interested in my needs, of course. To him I was just a vaginal playground, *I was just a sex object*! I'm thankful that I had the strength to leave him, to exercise my sexual rights, to find my sexual fulfillment. . . ."

Other women spoke of polymorphous sexuality, total body-play, open marriage, the techniques of masturbation.

And there was Betty Dodson.

"I've tried everything," said Betty Dodson, "from abstinence to marriage, which turned out to be, for me . . . abstinence." (laughter and applause) "Now, I'm a total sex freak. A few years ago people said, 'What do you want to be?' I said, 'I want to be a pervert. I want to be one of those sex fiends.' I was so straight and so turned off and so rigid in my proper role for so many years that after I got a divorce I cut loose and I continued that process right on. Now I'm indeed outrageous, but it's really a lot of fun. I feel better than I have ever felt and my sex life is incredible."

Madeline cheered along with the rest, clutched Lorna's hand, whispered, "I've got to talk to her."

A lot of people wanted to talk to Betty Dodson, though: This enigma with the paintbrush hair, curious unisex attire, and inspirationally brazen manner (who was not only a self-proclaimed sex freak but the artist who had prepared the slide show on female genitalia which was one of the most noted conference features, and who had designed as well the poster advertising this event, appropriately showing a brave, open, totally exposed and fearlessly androgynous nude woman against the background of a stylized vagina), and Betty Dodson could do no more than briefly nod in the direction of this young Indiana woman who seemed to follow her from workshop to workshop.

The workshops in and of themselves were overwhelming, of course. Sexual Fantasies. Women Loving Women. The Politics of Lesbianism. The Double Standard. Utopian Forms of Sexuality. Lorna remained quiet, Madeline asked constant questions. At Women Loving Women, for instance, she naively demanded, "But how is it possible for a heterosexual woman, or any woman, to consider a lesbian experience?" to receive the matter-of-fact reply that, "Heterosexual women aren't attracted to *every* man they meet; in fact the percentage of men a woman would agree to sleep with would be relatively low. It takes a special chemistry with either men or women. Some men you're attracted to, not all. And if you change your programming and open yourself to the possibility of sleeping with a woman, you eventually find some women you're attracted to."

That made sense. It all made sense. Madeline took notes, furiously, copiously. She continued to look for Betty Dodson, losing Lorna in the process, but managing to talk to a few workshop leaders, including an older woman whose droll attitude toward the precepts of the conference (precepts so new and strange to Madeline) provoked something approaching infatuation in the younger woman. The older woman was a lesbian, but not a totally "woman-identified woman."

"I'm bisexual," she said casually.

Fascinated, Madeline asked her, "Will you be at the party tonight?" feeling as she asked a surge of some strange light feeling ("as though I'd just asked her for a date," she would tell Lorna later).

"Probably—most everybody will be."

It was all swirling together in Madeline's head, later, when Lorna finally found her at the party and suggested they leave. Even in a relatively quiet corner it was difficult for Lorna to catch all of Madeline's words ("all so different here . . . CR would work for me here, I know . . . no female eunuchs here, just female warriors . . . if only there were some way I could stay here for a while. . . .") but what was clear was that Madeline didn't want to leave the party yet, and something in her friend's tone of voice made Lorna nervous. And when Madeline hadn't returned to the hotel by midnight, Lorna placed a call to Jerry, hesitantly preparing him for the possibility that Madeline might not be coming back to Hammond. "Have her call me the minute she gets in," said Jerry.

Madeline called, at 3 A.M., but her defense was ready. After all, if he were away on a business trip and needed to prolong his stay, he'd be right to do so. Well, she, Madeline, was in the business of living, of finding herself, and she was staying for a while.

"Besides, you can't pretend you want me back as a wife, just as a mother; but Timmy is your child too and you'll just have to be responsible for him for a while." If Jerry could send some money, fine; otherwise, Madeline would stay with "a friend I met tonight."

"Male or female?" Jerry asked somewhat caustically.

"Jerry," Madeline answered dryly, patiently, teacher-to-student, removed from her husband's disembodied voice not just by one thousand miles but by light-years of new knowledge, "to a sexually emancipated woman, that question is irrelevant."

"I'll send some money," Jerry said tiredly. "Have your way."

So Madeline remained, finding a small room on West

13th Street, with two clear goals in mind: to find sexual fulfillment (of course), and to join the movement which was working to bring sexual enlightenment to other women.

She never fully succeeded in becoming part of the movement in this vanguard city, however. Only occasionally did she establish real friendships; and her sexual contacts came mostly from sources other than feminism: a swinger's club, and casual pickups. (And in fact as time went on she relied more on casual meetings. Within the swinger's group, even the most adventurous genitals tended to be attached to minds sufficiently middle-class to be taken aback by Madeline's textbook feminist militancy: Such statements as "The problem with the sexual revolution is persistent male ignorance of clitoral stimulation" somehow worked against her continuing acceptability within this group.)

She found at least a few lovers through the women's movement, though, and these few provided experiences she counted among her most satisfying. One man, married to an acquaintance of Madeline's in NOW but living separately from his wife ("That gives us something in common," said Madeline as she invited him over) made her feel "charged, ready to explode" for hours on end, then skillfully caused all the explosions. And there was a woman who, following a Gay Women's Alliance rap session, came to Madeline's small room at the edge of the Village and stayed for several days: The two remained in bed most of that time, occasionally getting up to do yoga exercises, phone a "sister" to share the joy of their experience, or telephone out for wine and pizza. That episode was really quite extraordinary, thought Madeline.

There were some less satisfying incidents. Perusing sex books at a noted Eighth Street bookshop, Madeline met a man who asked her to accompany him to his apartment, explaining reassuringly, "I'm not a pervert or a rapist." He wasn't. He was very gentle. But after he brought her to orgasm a number of times through a variety of techniques, including use of a vibrator, he suddenly got up from the bed, sprang to the next room, and began typing. Madeline wandered after him and asked what was going on. Without breaking his rhythm on the keyboard, he explained that he was a writer—specializing in reporting sexual experiences. He was simply recording her responses and reactions while they were still fresh in his mind.

Madeline wondered as she dressed whether that might not be some sort of exploitation, but if so she'd fix him. Going directly home, she wrote out notes on *his* performance, had them Xeroxed, and mailed a copy to him, saving the originals for her own files.

On the whole, though, Madeline felt very emancipated. True, there were bouts of loneliness, but her CR group was helping her work that through. The group members provided more practical help too: They advised her to visit the women's clinic for VD checks, to be more careful in her contacts, to take a self-defense course.

Madeline tried to keep her sexual adventures consistent with her feminism; she tried as well to actively work with NOW and other groups, but remained always on the periphery of meaningful actions. She was somewhat irresponsible about committee work and meetings, due to a greater preoccupation with finding sex partners.

Much of her time seemed spent writing long, elaborate letters to her husband and acquaintances back home, in attempts to justify her decision not to return. One letter read, in part, "I should never have gotten married or had a child. Because I fell into a trap laid out for me, should I then live out my life in that trap? Of course not. I have to search for a new way of life, and I can do this only with other women, in an atmosphere where everyone's vision of me is uncontaminated by guilty stereotypes such as 'runaway mother.' " Madeline had rather quickly reached a point where she presented herself simply as an unattached woman, never mentioning a husband and child. References to her former life were only hints: ("Can you imagine, I used to spend half my time growing flowers. . . .")

Her letters quoted movement literature at length, but often to no point. *I want to consider how a woman's role as a wife and a socializer of children acts as a stunting influence upon her creativity,"* began one letter, which then went on merely to ask politely about Timmy, the weather in Hammond, and former neighbors.

Her husband, after trying several times to convince her to return, gave up. He hadn't really expected to succeed. His effort was perfunctory; the memory of their life together had a heavy sense of unreality to him. He requested a divorce, and she did not contest it. Madeline was alone.

Madeline caused worry in some of the women whom she met, particularly those few who knew the story of her marriage, her abrupt departure from it, her present sex-centered way of living. One of the Sexuality Conference facilitators was incredulous to learn of Madeline. "How on earth could anyone make such a drastic life-style change just on the stimulus of one conference?" she wondered. Though Madeline was not the only woman she knew of who had come to the conference from out of town and simply not gone home, Madeline was the only one she knew of who'd been married. How many such women were there? the facilitator wondered aloud. Probably not many; still, the fact that there were *any* gave her pause.

She acknowledged no responsibility, though, and

probably rightly so. "We can't be responsible for these inordinate hungers society builds up in women by denying them so many components of their identity. And then too, we expect adults to come to these conferences, not children."

Madeline was behaving somewhat like a child—taking all her answers from the books and literature, never bothering to ask if the questions had been properly posed.

Her CR sisters urged her to get a job, pointing out that there were areas to liberation besides sexual freedom. But Madeline seemed disinclined to look for work, at least as long as she could live meagerly on the small amount of money Jerry, out of some sense of duty or loyalty or pity or guilt or simply memory, continued to send to her each week.

Between sexual adventures, she read the movement literature, took notes; attended lectures, took more notes; and each weekend refined her filing system. She spent days pondering a copy of Shere Hite's sexuality questionnaire which she had found on the literature table at the NOW office. She wrote and rewrote her answers.

She made special efforts to meet some feminist leaders, often but not always with hopes for a sexual relationship. She wanted to get to know the Sexuality Committee chairperson; the founder of Gay Women's Alliance; the man who wrote a book on role-free sex; Shere Hite; and Betty Dodson (much as, years before, she had wanted to get to know the debate captain, the yearbook editor, the football quarterback).

In some inchoate way, she knew she was not living an integrated, mature life. At the Duchess, a movement bar, she told a friend one night, "Sometimes I feel like I'm still living through adolescence—I'm doing just what I did in high school, just studying and dating." The thought depressed her; she was quiet for a minute. Then she brightended. "Oh well," she said, "at least it's better than being a stupid, bored, frustrated, anonymous housewife living someplace like Hammond, Indiana."

She looked at her companion seriously. "Isn't it?" she asked.

The last time I saw Madeline was at a Women's Martial Arts Center demonstration and songfest in New York City in December of 1974. Women were being exhorted by the center director to "think like fighters, not victims," were told that street fighting requires being ready to put thumbs in eye sockets, poke the solar plexus, cup hands and hit ears to break the eardrums, push up on an attacker's chin with palm of hand, press against the artery in the back of the neck to produce unconsciousness, and "go for the groin. . . ." ("Don't grab the penis, though," the instructor said in an aside, "which is not that sensitive to pain. . . . Go for the testicles, which *are*. . . .")

Later, Margaret Sloan sang tenderly,

> *I want to make love with you,*
> *Cause you're a woman and I am too*
> *I want to make love with you,*
> *Not "to" you or "at" you, as men do. . . .*

Finally, in the last and most dramatic demonstration of the evening, kendo demonstrators, encased in gloves, helmets, and body padding, wielding bamboo rods and shouting violently, were reproved after their exhibition of feudal Japanese fighting by an angry feminist in a red work shirt who declared, "Long skirts are a symbol of female oppression: Why are you wearing long skirts?"

The explanation that the flared garment (actually culottes) worn on the lower body by kendo fighters serves a specific strategic purpose (to conceal foot movements of the fighters which might otherwise disclose their combat strategy) *and* that the garment was historically correct, having been worn by both women *and* men in feudal Japan, failed to assuage this particular feminist's indignation.

"Long skirts are a symbol of female oppression," Madeline repeated again, insistently, as though she had learned a lesson from some textbook somewhere, and had learned the lesson well.

The Search for Sex

Sex is an institution. It is also a drag.
—**Issue Number 8 of** *Rat* **(a feminist journal)**

*No doubt the most far-reaching hypothesis
extrapolated from these biological data is the
existence of a universal and physically normal
condition of woman's inability ever to reach complete
sexual satiation in the presence of the most intense,
repetitive orgasmic experiences, no matter how
produced. Theoretically, a woman could go on having
orgasms indefinitely, if physical exhaustion did not
intervene.*[1]
—**Mary Jane Sherfey, M.D.**

*The vaginal orgasm is just another thing they try to
sell you.*
—**New York radical feminist in private conversation**

*If it were true that we needed sex from men, it would
be a great misfortune, one that might almost doom
our fight. Fortunately, it is not true.*[2]
—**Dana Densmore**

Once women weren't supposed to talk of sex. Perhaps it's evidence of liberation that now we talk and hear and read of little else; and we're all to be eager players in this game and we're obliged to announce what team we're on (heterosexual, heterosexual monogamous, lesbian, political lesbian, bisexual) and count our orgasms and assess our skill according to the latest expert's score card.

An essay by Alix Shulman, "Organs and Orgasms," perhaps significantly, begins, "This essay is not about love-making. . . . Rather it is about genital relations, and how they have adversely affected the lives of women. The myths and lies about female genital anatomy are so wide-spread and so harmful to women that the subject deserves an altogether separate consideration."[3]

Germaine Greer and Kate Millett were the most vocal and best-publicized superstars of the movement for women's sexual emancipation, the most prominent dis-mantlers of "myths and lies" regarding female sexuality*: Millett attacked the stereotypes of exploited, subjugated, sexually humiliated women in literature; Greer objected to the real-life stereotype of the passive, soft, helpless, ac-quiescent, sexually unassertive female—regretting that we no longer subscribe to the notion of "the heated lust"of the female or consider the vagina a "vigorous" organ like the penis, and thus make of women sexual castrates, eunuchs.

But the real myth-breaker and liberator of female sex-uality was a woman named Anne Koedt. Anne Koedt was a founder of the radical movement in New York (New York Radical Women, New York Radical Feminists, The Feminists) and an editor of the annual *Notes*.† Koedt's con-tribution to the New Testament of Feminism was "The Myth of the Vaginal Orgasm," Section 1 of which first ap-peared in *Notes*, 1968. The entire article, based on infor-

---

*There is no intention here of presenting Greer and Millett as a team or even as colleagues within the movement. Reaction to the two varied widely, in fact, with Millett far more respected within the women's community for the integrity and exhaustive scholarship of her study. Feminists and radical feminists alike, however, looked askance at Greer, were put off by her flirtatious attitude toward the media, uncer-tain of how to take her lusty pursuit of the male sex, and questioned her self sexploitation. Claudia Dreifus was even moved to remark that "If Germaine Greer did not exist, Norman Mailer would have had to invent her."

†The most relevant writings of radical feminism were collected in 1968 and published under the title *Notes From the First Year*. *Notes From the Second Year* followed in 1970 and *Notes From the Third Year* in 1973

mation from Masters and Johnson studies and Mary Jane Sherfey's "A Theory of Female Sexuality," was first presented as a paper at the first national women's liberation conference, held Thanksgiving weekend that year in Chicago. It was printed in full in 1970 in *Notes* and by now has been reprinted in, excerpted from, or referred to in countless feminist anthologies and periodicals.

The importance of this document to the women's movement should not be underestimated. Basically, its argument ran as follows:

> —Male physicians and psychiatrists (notably, Freud and his followers) insisted that females have two kinds of orgasms, clitoral and vaginal. The clitoris, or outer area, is the site of the orgasm for the *immature* female. But when a woman matures and begins to have intercourse with men, she should develop a capacity for vaginal orgasm, in response to the thrusting of the penis.
> —Actually, the clitoris is a richly sensitive area, the vagina is not. The clitoris is constructed to achieve orgasm, the vagina is not. The so-called vaginal orgasm *simply does not exist.*
> —Men found the idea of the vaginal orgasm convenient, because men have the greatest satisfaction given friction with the vagina, not the clitoral area, which is external and not able to cause friction with the penis the way penetration does. Women have thus been defined sexually *in terms of what pleases men.*
> —Since women were supposed to have vaginal orgasms, and obviously could not, many women pretended to, thus causing incredible psychic strain and sometimes psychosis. Or, if they didn't pretend to have vaginal orgasms, they were defined as frigid and forced to think of themselves as inadequate or insufficiently feminine women.
> —Once scientific facts were known about the insensitiv-

ity of the vagina to stimulation, the myth of the vaginal orgasm nonetheless continued to be maintained by the (male) medical and scientific community because men prefer sexual penetration and fear they will become sexually expendable if the clitoris is substituted for the vagina as the center of pleasure for women.

In sum, the definition of feminine sexuality as vaginal was simply part of keeping women down; of making them sexually, as well as politically and socially and economically, subservient. Radical women responded to this information with predictable anger at having been cheated, deceived, victimized, denied their own sexual nature. They by and large agreed with Koedt that,

> We must redefine our sexuality. We must discard the "normal" concepts of sex and create new guidelines which take into account mutual sexual enjoyment. While the idea of mutual enjoyment is liberally applauded in marriage manuals, it is not followed to its logical conclusion. We must begin to demand that if certain sexual positions now defined as "standard" are not mutually conducive to orgasm, they no longer be defined as "standard." New techniques must be devised which transform this particular aspect of our current sexual exploitation.[4]

To this point, Koedt's approach was unarguably rational, the goal of "mutual sexual enjoyment" a desirable and positive one: The only problem was that if the marriage manuals Koedt referred to had given only lip service to the aim of *mutual* sexual enjoyment while functionally defining sexual techniques that aimed only at *male* enjoyment, conversely "mutual sexual enjoyment" would become an empty phrase to feminists who would counter tradition by seeking *female* enjoyment as an almost exclusive goal. Perhaps a clue to this development could have been intuited from such words as "demand" and "must be" and other phrases with connotations of militancy.

In any case, new techniques, new attitudes, new definitions were indeed to be devised, as of course were new positions to be recommended. Immediately, the missionary man-on-top position was condemned as male chauvinist in nature, offering little clitoral stimulation to the female. To accept it was mere pandering to an egoistic male desire for symbolic dominance: "Beyond the feminist talk about the myth of the vaginal orgasm lies a radical resentment of their position in the sexual act,"[5] wrote Sally Kempton; "Sexually emancipated women have long sung the praises of the female-superior position," instructed Greer; and one feminist periodical conveyed the spirit of the new orthodoxy in its title: *Off Our Backs*.

But if the vaginal orgasm had been a myth, the clitoral orgasm—*the* orgasm—was accepted overnight as a major verity. There are periods of time when myths are broken down, and usually the breaking-down process takes a while; but Koedt's impact was instant, her seeming single-handed victory over decades of Freudian thought an astonishing example of the speed with which change of thought can occur in a mass-media society.

And following Koedt's essay and its wide distribution, other papers appeared: "The Politics of Orgasm," "Organs and Orgasm," "The Search for Good Sex," and others. Anselma Del'Olio proclaimed in *Ms.* that male ignorance of women's need for clitoral orgasm was "the Achilles heel of the sexual revolution"; Alix Shulman added that of course men could never plead ignorance again

> if, from the beginning, their sex education went something like this:
>
> *Boy:* What's the difference between boys and girls?

> *Mother*: Mainly their sex organs. A boy has a penis and a girl has a clitoris.
> *Boy*: What's a clitoris?
> *Mother*: It's a tiny sensitive organ on a girl's body about where a penis is on a boy's body. It feels good to touch, like your penis.
> *Boy*: What's it for?
> *Mother*: For making love, for pleasure.

and concluded her essay with an injunction to women to *"Think clitoris."*[6]

And just as women, after Caroline Bird's *Born Female* and Friedan's *Feminine Mystique*, had become as sharp-eyed accountants, reviewing the ledgers of their life styles; summing up economic and domestic injustices, the raises not received, the dishes washed, the hours wasted in housework, idle passivity, or consumerism; women were now to turn their attention to yet another debit column, where the number of orgasms they hadn't had could be totalled.

It was thus after Koedt's essay that sex became political, and the orgasm was co-opted straight from the male value system, as a status symbol, like a corner office. Typical in tone is an essay by Sheila Cronan:

> Fifteen to twenty percent of all [American] married women have never had an orgasm. About fifty percent reach orgasm on a "now and then" basis. Meaning that they experience full culmination about one sex act out of three. Thirty to thirty-five percent of American wives say they "usually" reach orgasm, meaning that they get there two out of three times or thereabouts. Only a very few women can claim that they have an orgasm every time they take part in sexual activities.[7]

Further, "We all know that intercourse without orgasm is at best a waste of time," stated Cronan. (She also used the words "boring" and "painful" to describe such climax-less intercourse.) Del'Olio concurred, regretting that "the majority of women have to *put up with* (our italics) relatively infrequent orgasms during sexual—*at least heterosexual* (our italics)—encounters."

She continued,

> Women shouldn't feel embarrassed to request their own satisfaction in intercourse. A man with some respect for himself and for you will not be turned off by your honesty. You may be the first woman who ever talked to him straight, and he may welcome the opportunity to clear up doubts of his own. And if he is turned off, you are well rid of him.[8]

Some wondered if such an arrogant, characteristically unfeminine attitude meant that the feminist impulse was basically antisexual; someone even based a book around this theme (*The New Chastity*, by Midge Decter). Nothing could have been further from the truth. The new feminist theories might have been antimale, or antimale chauvinist, perhaps even anti*hetero*sexual, but there was no rejection of the idea of sexuality as a broad-based goal; instead, there was a noticeably active pursuit of sexuality, albeit in nontraditional ways.

A change of mood among these new female sex-seekers was unmistakable: from passivity to pursuit, from acquiescence to assertion. Men had always had orgasms, men had traditionally been the active, aggressive, initiating partners. Thus perhaps a liberated woman should also take it as her right to suggest or initiate—or demand.

Her attitude during the sex act itself should change too. A speaker at the NOW Sexuality Conference advised that for women, sex should be "strength and power . . . not feeling afraid. . . . It should have a lot in common with the martial arts. . . . Without a feeling of *virility*, a necessary component of female sexuality is missing."

Typifying this new injunction to genital gymnastics was one young woman taking part in the speak-out at the same conference:

> The new thing that I've added to sex has been Kung Fu, a martial art, and I have gotten into the whole body trip. It's one of the most exhilarating things I've done in my life. I've developed my muscles. . . . I've got very thin tapered muscles rippled all down my stomach and into my legs. When I'm doing Kung Fu I've got my pelvis forward, which is the motion for sex and not with the pelvis locked back. So Kung Fu has improved my body mobility in sex. If you're going to be a sexual person, you have got to be strong. . . . You can build strength through masturbation, through a martial art, through yoga, or exercise. And so this has been my odyssey. . . . One of my goals is to be a sexual athlete.[9]

A corollary to the proposal that women become stronger and more athletic sexually was the occasional suggestion that men become weaker, gentler. Feminist Andrea Dworkin advised that men should learn to make love "like women, using only the hands and mouth, and ejaculating through a flaccid penis." What she was after, she said, was "the transformation [of the sexual act] into androgyny."[10]

This was of course consistent with the radical feminist view that

> the world as it now exists is based on the corrupt notion of "maleness vs. femaleness." The oppression of women is based on this very notion and its attendant habits and institutions. We must eradicate the sexual divisions on which our society is based.[11]

Notions of "maleness vs. femaleness" had of course characterized the behavior of men and women, particularly in situations of courting, mating, cohabitation, and sexual union, with "male" role behavior exhibiting strength and power, "female" *surrendering* to that strength and power.

But if woman had traditionally surrendered, she had also seduced; and female seductiveness was part of the "corrupt" sex-role division since it represented only negative or indirect power, a corrupted and distorted form of assertion. It reinforced an undesirable concept of woman as wily, subtle, indirect. Traditional ways in which women communicated desire for a man, a willingness to be intimate with him (by look or touch or dress or gesture, or perhaps a look *at* the man combined with a suggestive touch of some nearby object) were lacking in forthrightness and therefore frowned on by feminists: The simple spoken word was preferred. A book on consciousness raising typically spoke with approval of a woman who might be said to be en route to androgyny:

> At the same time she was learning to assert herself at home. "I can tell you a big difference. Before, if I wanted to make love, I'd simply take a shower, put on perfume, and wear a sexy nightgown. Oh, my husband got the idea and loved it all right. It always made me feel a little ashamed somehow. Now I simply tell him what I want."[12]

Greer decried "passive ritualization," "the aching facial muscles brought on by the obligatory smiles," the "characterless passivity of the female" in courting situations. She would "by-pass the innuendo and short-circuit the whole process."

Now if the passivity of the female in courting situations might be described as characterless, there is nonetheless the chance that it persists because it is *functional*. Without probing too deeply into the complicated questions of the genesis of behavior patterns (biological versus societally engendered) it can yet be simply pointed out that certain human gestures—whether innate or not; whether instinct, impulse, or drive—are in any case cross-cultural.

Whatever our race or sex, shape of body or color of skin, and no matter at what time during history we have lived, we hold certain actions and responses in common with every other human being who has ever lived: We all stamp our feet when angry, bare our teeth when in a true rage, cover the lower part of our face with our hands when embarrassed, and raise our eyes to greet someone we recognize.

And though certain of these responses may have become illogically structured by various societies into an artificial male-female code, *these specialized responses too* have a basic commonality and predictability. In his arresting study, *Love and Hate: The Natural History of Behavior*, Eibl-Eibesfeldt reports that "regressive" behavior is noted in women cross-culturally when they wish to elicit affectionate behavior from a man, *e.g.*, when they wish to seduce.

Such regressive behavior includes lowering of the head and raising the eyes, as in a childish appeal; tongue signals; use of diminutives in speech; and pretended helplessness. The author terms these behaviors a "natural repertoire." If indeed *natural*, this repertoire suggests a female *nature* with a significant element of passivity.[13]

A number of references similar to Eibl-Eibesfeldt's could easily be gathered; yet even given a substantial collection of such references, few would insist that any firm conclusion be drawn, and fewer still would suggest that even if such patterns were inherent female "nature" they would be immutable, or that change would be necessarily undesirable.

Yet whether or not these behaviors have any sort of biological base or rest in any way on preprogramming,* experience still suggests that we have become habituated to such behaviors; and even granting that the transformation of woman from helplessly seducing and surrendering to a role more complete and assertive would be a good idea, the hoped-for "transformation into androgyny" of men and women is in for some transitional problems. Simply put, whether or not the aggressive/submissive, active/passive dichotomy of behaviors between male and female is biologically based or not, we seem to be having some trouble getting away from it.

The new female aggressiveness, as reflected by women's responses to feminist Shere Hite's *Sexual Honesty* questionnaire, shows attempted role change to be replete with problems:

"Unfortunately sex for me is like a fight. . . ."

"I have actually disgusted certain men, yes, turned them off by daring to satisfy myself."

"It is all very complex. I know if I was submissive all the time in bed he would come to my bed more often. I just

---

*Some feminists, Firestone included, seem to accept the possibility of biologically based behavior differences, even though considering them ultimately irrelevant: Firestone would argue that "the 'natural' is not necessarily a 'human' value. Humanity has begun to outgrow nature." Other feminists condemn the very possibility that nature designed female dependency. Anthropologist Evelyn Reed, for example, calls the notion that "nature [is] responsible for having condemned females to prehistoric helplessness" mere "pernicious pseudoscientific propanganda."

can't bring myself to do it anymore. It represents, perhaps, my unwillingness to be submissive in our interactions *out* of bed."[14]

Even Susan Lydon in her important essay "The Politics of Orgasm" admitted that the prospect that "a woman could seek her satisfaction as aggressively as a man sought his" was "a prospect which didn't appeal to too many men." Male lack of enthusiasm for the new androgyny was noticeable enough to provoke many evenings of derision among Chicago feminists in early 1973. One woman drew general laughter with a pointed rhyme:

> *My expectations are rising,*
> *I demand good sex when I ball,*
> *Therefore it is unsurprising*
> *That* he *ceases to uprise at all.*

The Lilith Manifesto both acknowledged and dismissed this problem by advising,

> If you, brother, can't get a hard-on for a woman who doesn't grovel at your feet, that's *your* hang-up; and sister, if you can't turn on to a man who won't club you and drag you off by the hair, that's yours. Keep your hang-ups the hell out of this revolution.[15]

Some feminists certainly viewed the problem in a more heartfelt way. The concept of androgyny in sex relations, with equal impulse and assertion on the part of man and woman, reflected after all the overriding feminist goal of independent personhood for women, of which sexual independence was only one aspect (albeit a troublesome one, the area where behavior was least inclined to bow to logic). Jane O'Reilly, for example, fancifully equating her own independent personhood with the ability to walk through walls, proceeded to admit that walking through bedroom doors seemed a somewhat different matter: "It comes as an annoying shock," she wrote,

> after all that effort and struggle, to discover that the ability to walk through brick walls is not a helpful talent when it comes to the hopelessly entangled, still remaining problems of love and sex. . . .
>
> Once . . . wafting spontaneously toward my bed, liberated at last, I heard a slow shuffle and an ominous rumble behind me. "Well, gee, do you act like this all the time? I mean, ugh, I don't usually . . . umm . . . let's just talk for a while. . . ."[16]

And if Ms. O'Reilly's personal ruminations on love and liberation and New Arrangements contain a few heartening experiences, there is also one startling regression to be found in her statement, "I think I have identified the problem. I need to get laid. . . . Damn it, I said *I want to get laid*."

Now, "laid" is not an androgynous verb, but rather one laden with connotations of layer/layee, of conquest/surrender—a nasty (or poignant, depending on one's point of view) echo of the old roles, the old rules.

More than a few women, it seems, are having trouble wrenching away from the old roles, or becoming attracted to the gentle, unassertive, respectful, androgynous man: Nora Ephron in the pages of *Esquire* confesses to fantasies of "faceless men who rip my clothes off "[17]; Ingrid Bengis in *Combat in the Erogenous Zone* writes, "When I meet a man who is kind but sexless, my interest ebbs; when I meet a man who is less than kind but sexually attractive, there is a struggle . . ."[18]; and even Sylvia Plath mourned that *"Every woman adores a Fascist, the boot in the face . . ."*[19] This last may be poetic overstatement, yet it well reflects the illogically lingering desire to be dominated that haunts many transitional women.

One moving example is recounted by a West Coast woman in an early issue of *Momma*, as she describes an affair with a man called Juan, "sulky, petulant, and mean . . ."

Now comes the story of our short life together, first the 10 weeks of courtship where I flew up to Bolinas every weekend while we waited for the semester to end. I was working, he wasn't, but he didn't like to fly. Some weekends I couldn't make it; he swore at me over the phone. One weekend he did come down, after many quarrels, and brought his son. He ranted, literally all weekend. My shrink looked more grim each week. I dumped my cheerful gentleman admirers and stayed home each night to wait for Juan's call—or to call him, since he was worried about his phone bill.

My ex-husband said, upon hearing that I was planning on quitting my job, leaving my house, and going north, "I don't know why you're doing it, Carolyn. Juan seems just like I am, only in spades." It was true, of course. . . . Once up in Bolinas: Juan and I made love all night and talked all day. We took long walks and went to the beach. He hated my cooking; he also didn't care about my writing. When a piece I did for *Esquire* came out, he said of course there would always be a market for women who talked dirty. When another of my oldest friends (who had gone out with him many years ago) tried to kill herself that summer, and wrote from the hospital pitifully requesting that she come up to the farm for a few days, he (remembering it was she who had broken off that particular relationship) said no, she "deserved to drown in her own muck." We were outside in his vegetable garden during this exchange, and when I heatedly disagreed, he squirted me with a hose. (I want to recall to the reader, and to myself at this point, that I am 38 years old, have a 165 IQ, a Ph.D., am a published novelist, and own an acre of land.) There is just no use in saying, *What happened to everything you knew? About equality, about not being a second-class citizen anymore.* My identity, my "accomplishments," my friends, my children, all went down the drain when I looked at him (or, God help me, when he touched me).[20]

Given that such experiences are not unique, it's not terribly surprising that many emerging feminists despair of attaining a truly egalitarian relationship with someone "groomed from birth to rule," and resolve, with regret or pride or some mixture thereof, *"I'm going to learn to live without a man."* A typical feminist workshop theme develops along the lines of: True sexual autonomy necessitates the woman herself as center and men secondary, peripheral, in fact expendable, particularly if political inequities contraindicate the relationship.

Accepting the principle of men expendable as partners offers potential for solution-by-avoidance of a lot of problems: Accepting male expendability, one can just put the dice back in the cup, fold up the board, and walk away from the entire game—or perhaps look around for other games. A body made strong by kung fu, after all, can find many sexual styles, among them self-sufficiency: autoeroticism. Submission? Dominance? Politically unacceptable fantasies? Subtle innuendo to men from women? All that just needn't matter anymore. What matters is just the *self*, distinct from any relationship.

Barbara Seaman, who elsewhere had written, modestly enough, "we [women] have been too shy about telling our lovers what we want," pointed out (on behalf of a radical friend) to a VIVA symposium, "If you tell a man what you like and ask him to do it, you're still handing over to him the responsibility for satisfying you. . . . The really autonomous thing to do is to just satisfy yourself."

Betty Friedan, rather incredulous, asked, "In other words, to masturbate?"

"Yes, while you're with him," was the idea, Seaman replied. "You know, like let him worry about himself."[21]

Carrying this premise one step further, why then even have him in bed with you?

If one accepts that the goal of sex is orgasm, that "intercourse without orgasm is at best a waste of time," the logical mind must then proceed to ask whether intercourse is the best way to reach that goal of orgasm.

According to Shere Hite, the author and editor of a unique sexuality questionnaire—to which two thousand readers of *Ms.*, *Mademoiselle*, *Bride's*, and the *NOW Newsletter* responded in detail—*it's not*.

"Almost without exception," Hite points out, "women indicate that intercourse fails to bring orgasm. 'I simply don't come from vaginal penetration' is a common response. Or women will break it down as 'During intercourse—never; masturbation—always; cunnilingus —almost always; manual stimulation by partner —sometimes.' It seems clear that intercourse is for many women an inefficient way to produce orgasmic satisfaction. More and better orgasms can be self-produced. Why do these women continue sleeping with men? It's not out of physical need; they certainly don't *need* to. . . ." A pause. "Well, eventually, maybe they'll figure that out."

Lesbianism and masturbation are two obvious alternatives to intercourse. Del Martin and Phyllis Lyon in *Lesbian/Woman* contend that after all "the act is the same, whether between members of the same sex or the opposite sex." And Martha Shelley in "Notes of A Radical Lesbian" proclaims that the act is superior in nature when performed by two women; decries "hasty and inept" encounters with men; declares that the penis is certainly no prerequisite to sexual pleasure. ("Man, we can do without it, and keep it going longer, too.")

The lesbian practice of tribadism is said to be particularly well suited to the achievement of orgasm or multiple orgasm, since it consists of two women rubbing their pubic areas together, one atop the other, thus achieving direct clitoral stimulation. Other lesbian sex styles include cunnilingus and mutual masturbation; and although these are heterosexual practices as well, homosexual women claim there is a difference: "Lesbians don't just hop to it, as some men do. Foreplay—embracing, kissing on the mouth and other parts of the body, breast fondling and sucking, nibbling at the ear, and touching and stroking various erogenous zones of the body—is important to lesbian sexuality," say Lyon and Martin.

The tenderness, the lack of prescribed roles, the comfort a woman can feel in bed with another person whom she has not been raised to believe to be foreign, profoundly different from herself, are all said to be conducive to the achievement of orgasm, too. In "Women Loving Women" workshops and in such books as *Lesbian/Woman* one hears frequently of women who only achieved orgasm when they began to sleep with those of their own sex.

And if one is serious about orgasm, one may join the thousands of women who utilize a Panasonic or an Oster or a Wahl or a Prelude 2, a Home Massager or a Swedish Stimulator—all guaranteed, their proponents say, to produce an orgasm as efficiently as toasters heat bread.

At one of NOW's noted sexuality conferences, the acceptability of such a device might be deduced from the heavy applause which greeted Betty Dodson's admission that:

> I'm probably hooked on my vibrator. I'm probably going steady with it, but I'll worry about that later. I don't know . . . that's the latest feedback I get. "You're hooked on your vibrator." And I say, "Listen, what can I say?" I've got four with me at the conference—*four!* Not one, I've got *four* vibrators and I mean it's like a groove. I change them over. Actually, the reason I do that is that they get hot and you have to change over to the next one. . . .[22]

Another woman read a poem called "Ode to a Vibrator," which elaborated on the theme of having at last been freed "from the consuming need to have a man." "You never have a headache when I need you most," one line said, and then went on to praise the gadget's unfailing potency to much laughter and applause.

Feminists with an antitechnological bias may come to regard simple masturbation as their primary sex style and mode of sexual release; although "simple" masturbation is at times approached as sport or skill or art. Betty Dodson, often called the Mother of Masturbation, is among several women on both coasts who are known in feminist circles for giving masturbation parties, which are intended to provide both exercise and, if necessary, education regarding techniques. "I can recall being hesitant at first about attending," reported one woman, "but I'm so glad I did. I remember the astonishment I felt at the first party when I realized I had been on the living room floor on my mat, pleasurably and comfortably masturbating for almost *one hour.* Oh, I had several orgasms, more than several, a good number. I'm going back of course. By the way, do you know the way that masturbation parties work? Each person has to get into his or her *own* masturbation trip. . . . You can use a vibrator or anything you want—except, of course, another person. A cucumber is fantastic!" Sometimes, she added, "homework" assignments are given: one had a romantic overtone, with participants instructed to enjoy a steak dinner with wine and candlelight—by themselves —before beginning masturbation.

It's not impossible to imagine that soon the popularity of masturbation manuals will rival that of sex manuals. (*The Joy Of . . .* , *Everything You Always Wanted to Know About . . .* may join the first book on masturbation, *For Yourself* by Lonnie Barbach, published, whimsically, on Valentine's Day 1975.) The possibility is real, because some women are approaching the subject with a scientific, analytical seriousness undreamt of by such as Philip Roth. One might consider, for a start, question number twenty-four of Shere Hite's *Sexual Honesty* questionnaire:

> "How do you masturbate? Please explain with a drawing or detailed description. For example, what do you use for stimulation—your fingers or hand or a vibrator, etc.? What kinds of motions do you like—circular, patting, up and down, etc.? Do you use two hands, or if not, what do you do with the other hand? Are the legs together or apart? Where do you touch yourself? Etc. What is the sequence of events when you masturbate? For example one person might put her legs together, then massage the clitoral area with her hand, while pushing the lips together rhythmically between her legs with the pelvis also moving slightly, etc."[23]

The answers were returned by the hundreds:

> "I stimulate my clitoris with the third finger of my right hand until I begin to feel excited. Then I use my left

hand to stimulate my nipples at the same time. . . . For
my clitoris, I usually use circular or back-and-forth
motions—very rarely patting motions for a short while. I
often find that I have to stop at intervals as though the
clitoris becomes desensitized by the friction, and I have
to let it build up sensitivity. . . . It seems I must have
my legs wide apart (knees bent out) and I have found that
if I can arch my back I am much more sensitive."

"I masturbate with my hand. I usually lie on my back but
sometimes on my stomach. . . . I have many different
movements. Flat of hand sideways across the entire
mons area, fingers alongside of the clitoris and then up
and down or sideways, circular movement with hands or
fingers. The movement is not so important as that a
rhythm be maintained and that the pressure be firm and
increasing in firmness until orgasm. . . . Legs
closed. . . ."

"Often I touch my face with my left hand. Sometimes I
kiss this hand. Almost always I masturbate with my right
hand only. . . . I use the middle two fingers of my right
hand lightly caressing the outer genital area. . . . No
other combination of fingers is as effective, versatile, or
comfortable. Parallel motion on the clitoris is not as effective as slow small circular motions at first, alternated
with rapid sideways motions with stronger pressure and
this alternated with vaginal penetration (by fingers) usually in a circular stroking, pressing hard on the walls of
the vagina and feeling its limitations. . . . At the end the
pressure must be very accurate, steady, rhythmic, very
fast, and not too hard. . . . I can come for three or four
seconds; it's most intense the first one or two seconds. I
have come as many as eleven times in twenty minutes

with the last several as close together as thirty
seconds. . . ."24*

One respondent compared masturbation to intercourse by explaining, "Orgasm during intercourse is
stronger emotionally, but for outright getting it done, me
wanting five or more orgasms, I can satisfy myself alone
better than with a man."

The utilitarian tone of such phrases as "for outright
getting it done" bespeaks a radical departure from all prior
concepts of female sexuality, implicitly defines orgasm as a
mere mechanistic release, and inappropriately localizes
female sexual response to the clitoris in exact imitation of
the mistaken thinking which would restrict male response
to the penis. "I use the middle two fingers of my right
hand . . . no other combination of fingers is as effective,
versatile, or comfortable . . ." One recalls a comment on
sex from an essay in *Notes from the First Year*: "Sometimes
one would rather play Ping-Pong." Small wonder.

There is a psychological process described by Freud
known as reaction-formation, showing itself as a strong
overt response or feeling which is precisely opposite to an
underlying wish, long since renounced or repressed: The
adult who craves spinach and shuns desserts may be showing reaction-formation toward a phase of childhood which
was conflicted in relation to food. In an expanded social

*The exhaustiveness of this questionnaire, and the thoroughness of the
responses, cannot fail to impress! Note that these quotes are excerpted
from even longer responses; and that, depending on which of two
forms of the questionnaire was used, there were either *fifty-seven* or
sixty-three questions to be answered. Shere Hite's report on this major
survey of women's personal testimony about their sexuality is a significant work, the first of its kind, and is published by Warner Paperback Library.

field, the Sexual Revolution and Puritanism might serve as examples of reaction-formation to each other: A characteristic lack of compromise between or integration of opposing forces is seen. And so too, orgasm obsession may be over-reaction to male chauvinism within the various professional spheres which touch on sexuality. That a predominantly male medical-psychiatric establishment ignored the sexual nature and needs of women until quite recently is beyond serious dispute. It is appallingly easy to find advice such as the following persisting into the early 1970s:

> I would say that in most cases when a man reaches orgasm before his partner it is not necessary for him to do anything about it. Why should he? After all, he's been sexually satisfied, and his wife can now turn over and get to sleep that much sooner. . . . Now seriously. Who makes all the fuss about female orgasmic response? Anyone who's ever had the fortune (?) to listen to a women's bridge club discuss such mundane matters can attest that most wives can take sex or leave it alone.[25]

One could of course also quote Freud and feel appalled, or Deutsch, or Marie Robinson, or even David Reuben, or any of a score of others whose biases on the sexual nature of the female have reached print or influenced thought. However, one might turn an equally skeptical eye to the current feminist preoccupation with the orgasm and wonder if it has not the quality of a fetish. Karen Horney's "tyranny of the shoulds" might apply equally well to Freud's insistence that a mature female should have vaginal orgasms and to the dicta of Koedt, Shulman, and others that females should have clitoral ones!

What has the orgasm come to represent? Political obligation or personal duty rather than civil right or biological release? Prerequisite rather than potential? Need rather than capacity? Are the feminist authorities on sex really presenting information in a manner that is relevant to women's lives today? Or, possibly, are the facts provided by Masters and Johnson, Sherfey and others becoming distorted—made to serve political goals that lie outside the realm of sexuality?

It is evident to some readers of Masters and Johnson that their research *to them* signalled no need for a militant crusade; that their major contribution was to identify orgasmic capacity, not need; that their most value-laden disclosures attested to variability, not insatiability, of the female. As part of their conclusion to *Human Sexual Response*, they wrote, "With orgasmic physiology established, the human female now has an undeniable opportunity to develop realistically her own sexual response levels."[26]

The "opportunity" is no doubt still there, though how "realistically" it has been developed thus far is open to individual interpretation.

To the extent that desire for sexual fulfillment confines itself to pursuit of orgasm, the refinement seems overly simple, unrealistic, and sufficient at times to force premature abandonment of (heterosexual) relationships that may have proved satisfying in other ways.

If it is legitimate for feminists to inform us that (a) women do have a healthy capacity/need for orgasm, and that (b) heterosexual intercourse is a comparatively inefficient way to achieve orgasm (compared to, say, a "scientific masterpiece of sweet vibrations"), what information is offered to those women who accept the implications of (a) but not of (b)? Who remain sufficiently nonradicalized as to prefer to sleep with men?

Orgasm achieved through intercourse seems typically somewhat slower than that resulting from manual stimulation: A study conducted in 1971 which I have seen nowhere refuted since indicates that if a woman has about twenty minutes of emotionally involved sexual foreplay with her lover, in the vast majority of cases (around 95 percent) she can and will attain an orgasm. The same study also found that if the male maintains the penis in the vagina for fifteen minutes or more only a very small percentage of women will fail to have an orgasm.

The woman whose conscious preference would be that sort of intercourse combined with foreplay (and why not *afterplay* as well as foreplay?) will find quotes from Koedt and Greer of little use. Fortunately, she may not need them (fortunately, some things still come naturally), but if such a woman should seek advice from a feminist information source, she'd not be apt to find it. Evidently a topic such as "Improving Sex Relations *Between* the Sexes" is sufficiently banal (or insufficiently political) for *Ms.* or *Off Our Backs*, and of the more than fifty workshops held at the last NOW Sexuality Conference, not one was devoted to mutual male-female satisfaction within an enduring relationship. (Twenty blocks away from the conference workshops sexual insights of quite a different nature were being sought in the Ingmar Bergman film, *Scenes From a Marriage*: re-encountering his former wife after their separation and her consequent sexual development, Johann asks Marianne poignantly, "Could you possibly ration your female strength?" Would a sexually emergent woman at the militant Sexuality Conference have even entertained such a question?)

The existence of the annual feminist Sexuality Conference per se is not the least regrettable or objectionable; the lack of integration of biological and psychological approaches is. Shere Hite's asking two thousand women "How do you masturbate . . ." is similarly unobjectionable, but could she not have asked as well, "*Why* do you . . ."? One does not mind Del'Olio's rather militant essay in *Ms.*, simply the parenthetical scorn with which she dismisses heterosexual relationships.

Why does there seem to be a feminist aversion to the option of heterosexual orgasmic satisfaction? Do feminists find orgasm a worthy goal, yet find orgasm with a man so contaminated with overtones of yielding or submission as to be intolerable? Do these same feminists thus tend to bolster themselves with an up-to-the-minute concept of the orgasm as a mere physical release which can be adequately provided by friction of any kind?

The limitation of sexuality to consideration of orgasm leaves something out—probably leaves several things out. Now that sex is supposedly a matter which can be openly discussed, one yearns for some impulsive, gut-level reactions on such occasions as sexuality conferences. (Amidst all the talk of counting and timing, why doesn't somebody simply yell, "Look, *orgasms are different*" or "Sometimes you don't *need* twenty!" This doesn't seem to be happening; in fact, it's not impossible that women are accepting Koedt with the same docility with which they accepted Freud, and are still going home to their private pretenses and their personal solutions.)

Surely there is more to sex than orgasm. As Mary Calderone has said, "After orgasm, what?" An orgasm is, after all, only an orgasm. It is not a dimension of personality. Other things can matter, too. Does not simple touching matter, or overtones of mood? What of factors of emotion, perceptions of difference, personal appreciation, the kinds of knowledge and giving that one's mind plays with during that time when a man and woman are naked with one another?

Can any of the sexual mythologies speak to us then without risk of disintegration of our new feminist identities—say the surge of some dim perception that the masculine form represents some principle of motion or initiation, the feminine principle meets, allows, transforms? Does it matter who initiates? Does it matter that there are probably some differences—is it possible that some of the differences enrich the situation rather than overcast it with oppression?

And surely there *are* differences, just a few, that were designed as part of no one's chauvinist plot. Newborn males (physicians tell us) often have an erection as they emerge from the womb; infant females do not lubricate until eight hours after birth. (Maybe "culturally corrupt notions of maleness vs. femaleness" instill in us a lot of nonsense, but culture can't be responsible for *that*.) Another unarguable difference (the sex researchers tell us) is that women after intercourse move closer to their partners *in sleep*, whereas men do not. Is that cultural design?

And at the heart of it, it *is* man who penetrates, woman who receives: And that must be biology, not culture; and some restless, dimly understood (and perhaps best *not* fully understood) perceptions of such differences can stir a desire for a more total aesthetic experience with another than just the physical release of orgasm.

An individual who reaches for a vibrator obviously has the limited goal of orgasm in mind. A man and woman who reach for one another probably do not. At that moment, the intense desire may be simply to see the other's body, to appreciate the texture of an area of skin, the swell of a muscle, the sweep of a line. To see and then to touch may in themselves be what is wanted. And whether great release or light feeling will result an hour later is not the point at all—what matters is that the act is not just deed, but gift.

Rollo May, in *Love and Will*, states his belief that

> We have been led astray to think that the aim of the love act is the orgasm. . . . The moment of greatest significance in love-making, as judged by what people remember in the experience and what patients dream about, is not the moment of orgasm. It is rather the moment of entrance, the moment of penetration of the erection of the man into the vagina of the woman. This is the moment that shakes us, that has within it the great wonder, tremendous and tremulous as it may be—or disappointing and despairing, which says the same thing from the opposite point of view. This is the moment when the person's reactions to the love-making experience are most original, most individual, most truly their own. This, and not the orgasm, is the moment of union and the realization that we have won the other.[27]*

Would feminism compromise itself too much by admitting the possibility that the orgasm is different for the female than the male . . . the possibility that, sometimes, sexual union without orgasm may be a pleasurable, indeed profound, experience. . . . the possibility that, sometimes, we go to bed for other reasons than to achieve a particular series of muscular spasms along some inner neural pathway?

---

*One is reminded both of the French poet who declared that in the act of sex "It is every beginning which is lovely," and of the American working-class wife who told sociologist Mirra Komarovsky, "Well, sure I don't always go off like a factory whistle, still it's almost always nice."

Sonia:

A Liberated Woman Leaves

a Liberated Marriage

Brian was sprawled in front of the fireplace, weight on one elbow, one knee up, holding a paper cup of wine, his face flushed from either the wine or the fire. He touched Sonia's shoulder tentatively with his toe to see if she was asleep, and she seemed to be. He lowered his voice slightly as he continued talking to Elaine and Joe, jovially recounting the interview he and Sonia had had at a television station that morning.

The television show had been much awaited in this small community. The topic—Radical Life Styles. Liberated Marriage.

"They had talked to us by phone, of course, but hadn't seen us. They expected us to be younger, I think, wilder, and maybe more radical looking. The producer's jaw dropped when he saw Sonia. She had her hair braided and pinned on top of her head, and her nose was windburned because she'd been out playing tennis earlier—I'd say the word for her was . . . *demure*. Yes, I'd say she looked as demure as . . . a farmer's wife or something. . . ." He nudged again, gently, with his toe, wanting a response, some small pretended outrage.

She, not quite asleep after all, murmured, "And you looked like that farmer," smiled, shifted her weight, closed her eyes again, content to let Brian tell the story.

"Yes, well, and they said they were surprised that I looked so masculine. Can you imagine them admitting a thing like that? What did they expect, a ninety-seven-pound weakling?"

"Well, what did they ask you?" Joe wanted to know.

"Predictable things at first. Why did we decide to switch roles for a year. Both interviewers could accept on principle that it's enriching, a creative learning experience for both of us to do this, but you could see they had some blocks. . . . They started showing their skepticism with little digs like, 'Do the children ever call you *Mommy*?' 'Do you wear an apron?' An *apron*!

"On and on. Had we written a contract? Were there any problems? Did I feel annoyed or ashamed or unmanly doing housework?

"Well, the truth is that I'm only now coming out of a severe hate-the-housework phase, and I'm afraid I didn't stress that enough on the show—how your self-image can drop, what awful things housework can do to your mind if you get hung up on the details. And there's another point I'm not sure I made fully—how inept I felt at first, how I remembered and envied how easily Sonia had done things."

"Of course my female genes gave me a natural advantage," put in a quiet voice from the floor.

"No, seriously, Sonia, there was—there really used to be a rhythm to the way you'd do things, the way the washing machine would toss its way through the old sheets as you put on the new ones; to the way you'd run up and down the stairs, even; and the way you'd straighten the dining room and set the table as the bread and whatever else was baking. Damnit, it's the *timing* I can't get right. Always with you the timing was perfect, the meal and the table ready together, not once do I recall it failing; and I swear it seemed you used to fold the sheets and do the kids' ironing at the same time; it was like a dance, it all worked so smoothly. . . .

"Ah damnit, the bread! I'm in a real trap about that bread, of course." Brian was rambling now, a little high. "With the mill right on our place, the miller coming once a week and giving us free flour if he can grind his wheat there, I don't have any choice but to bake our own; besides, we got so used to Sonia's home-baked bread, not one of us can tolerate the other stuff—not even the birds will touch it. . . . So there I am, every morning, punching dough . . ."

"Well, all that flour," Elaine laughed. "Maybe I *will* just have to give you an apron, Brian." Her voice was warm and loving.

Brian hooted, poured more wine. "Sure," he said good-naturedly. "It can replace the shawl I used to wear when I was stuck in an office being a frustrated assistant principal. . . ."

The shawl was a private joke among the four of them: The first year they all had known each other, they had at Christmas deemed Brian a "grumpy old man" and given him a shawl that Elaine had made, with a note urging him to now indulge in "comfortably huddled irascibility."

"Yes, I think I'm going to put that shawl away for good now." Brian was in a rare, expansive mood tonight; but his expansive moods were not quite so rare now as formerly, and that pleased Sonia, who had wanted for so long to find ways to make Brian more open with others, freer to let himself be known. . . .

The change of role responsibilities had helped a lot. Brian was really happier at home, working quietly in the afternoons in his den, among the reference books and periodicals, preparing papers for conferences; he had always hated the intricate bureaucracies surrounding social work, whereas Sonia took to the situation with a simple zest, unraveled the intricacies as quickly as possible, then got to her case loads.

"And then when I told them how we'd met—in the *chapel* at the University of Georgia—it completely blew their stereotype!" Brian smiled, remembering, probably, not the interview that morning but quite a different morning, a Sunday thirteen years before, when he had met the girl now drifting in and out of sleep beside his feet.

Sonia—dark, lean, dynamic, outgoing, with a quiet sense of vividness and energy—seemed Brian's opposite in so many ways and therefore precisely suited to so many of his needs. Brian was thoughtful and studious, rugged —almost athletic—in appearance, yet with a reserved manner that was almost mysterious at times. His intelligence was a match for Sonia's own keen mind, his dormant sense of humor awakened by her consistent good nature. Sonia, it seemed, was always smiling.

They were drawn to each other physically, these two nineteen-year-old sophomores, in a way that neither had ever been drawn to another before.

Sonia's background and upbringing were severely religious, proscriptions against early sexual activity predictable: "Remember a boy needs to respect a girl, and furthermore no grown man ever wants 'used goods,' " her father moralized. "Sunny, I don't *ever* want to see you come home from a date with your blouse wrinkled," her mother added, more practically.

Actually, neither Sonia nor Brian had ever done more than kissed at the end of a date—and Brian hadn't done much of that. He hadn't always had his present, sturdy build. His delicacy and studiousness and docility had caused some grade-school classmates (with that attitude of unerring cruelty peculiar to children of a certain age and insecurity) to nickname him Bri-*ann*.

The effects of this had lingered somehow through adolescence, leaving him wary of school social events, and shy of girls to the point of semiseclusion. Only when he left New England for the University of Georgia did he suddenly find himself among those with whom he had no prior history: On his natural merits he was respected, accepted by others—even somewhat sought after. *Well, all right*, he thought, and flourished.

By the time he met Sonia, he had a firmly rooted positive feeling of himself; he was confident enough to think that although she was one of the most popular girls on campus, that he somehow deserved her.

She thought so too, and loved instantly not just the veneer of confidence but the hesitancies and insecurities that had so lately been a part of him, and were still so close beneath the surface of his manner, and which only she saw, and sought to strengthen.

Friends watched Sonia and Brian with some jealousy, more joy. Popular interpretation had it that three other couples fell in love and got engaged when Sonia and Brian did, for no better reason than that they were suffused with the reflected glow of this couple's warmly joined compatibilities.

And then they married (with two ceremonies, one in Sonia's home-town church where they promised to "love, honor and obey . . . till death do us part," and again at the campus chapel where they spoke their own vows, "To honor and cherish, to treasure and nurture, so long as the beauty of the love we now know holds firm and sure within our hearts,"), and after they married they waved to those with whom they'd shared four years or more and drove north and east toward whatever future lay in that direction, on an all-summer honeymoon odyssey, in a British racing green Griffith, a wedding present from Sonia's parents.

The year was 1965, and the world seemed safe then for couples such as they: If God had died, idealism had not; liberalism flourished modestly even in this part of rural Georgia; there was still assumed to be a future; and the best-selling book on their campus that semester was *The Prophet*, which Brian gave to Sonia as a wedding present, and the two were indeed "believers in life and the bounty of life"; and it was spring.

They camped out on Ocracoke Island, swam at Virginia Beach, bemoaned the poverty of the feeble towns along the North Carolina side roads, were touched by the awe with which the children of any of these towns were drawn to their Griffith, sometimes asking hesitantly if they might touch the low hood or wire wheels. . . . They visited Resurrection City, talked of VISTA or the Peace Corps, made friends wherever they stopped or stayed ("We'll get in touch with you if we go through Norfolk; we won't forget"). And when they saw the rolling hills and sun-drenched vistas of Bucks County, Pennsylvania, they silently reached for each other's hand without taking their eyes from the hills, and knew this was the place that they'd call home. . . .

Those hills looked little different then than when an Irish homesteader named Jamie Brady had surveyed them almost two centuries before. The difference was that Jamie Brady had built, stone by stone and rough-hewn log by rough-hewn log, the four-story hillside dwelling that would now belong to Sonia and Brian—for a while—and where their children would be born.

Brian and Sonia were not mere typical starry-eyed newlyweds selecting their first home according to *House and Garden* specifications. The architecture of this place was larger ("With twenty rooms, we'd need a magazine called *Castle and Countryside* as a guide for decorating," quipped Sonia) and the architecture of their life together was to be larger too: educational administration for Brian, school counseling for Sonia, self-fulfillment and productivity for both. Of course, Sonia's work would be part-time. Of course, Sonia would see to the care of this historic house.

It was, after all, only 1965.

The editors of *House and Garden* might have approved, however, of the style and mood of the place: early American antiques, some cabinets and reproductions handmade by Brian, the grain in the old Brady mill on the property, horses neatly stabled just a short walk from the tennis courts, apples and popcorn always laid out by the open hearth in the kitchen . . . but *House and Garden* writers, when, in fact, they came to consider a story on the house and spent a week with Sonia and Brian, were somewhat bemused by the twentieth-century activity that swirled in and out of the eighteenth-century dwelling. The discussions around that fireplace were sometimes radical, the discussants often imported from nearby Washington, D.C.; New York; and farther. Friends from college were now in government staff jobs with great potential for reform, and one worked with Ralph Nader. Evenings, one spoke of guaranteed incomes, electoral reform, civil rights, the people's lobby, militant consumer-action programs —and sometimes even alternatives to marriage.

The children came, completing the picture: delicate

Kristen and, one year later, bawling, lusty Dan. Lucky infants. Their first perceptions were of singing sycamores and pines, the quiet mill and stream. Kristen's first tangible memory was of The Party (actually one of many), which she observed on a summer evening from the balcony of her white-and-yellow second-story bedroom. She saw about forty adults divide into Red and Blue teams and behave much like children as they participated in a treasure hunt Sonia had planned over many days.

Kristen was two years old, and it was 1969.

"In what ethereal dances, by what eternal *streams*," read one clue for the Blue team, which led to many bare foot and wet cuff, while Red searched for a "needle*point* in a haystack" clue and after finding it read small tapestry letters instructing, "Hurry, for the *elms* fade into dimness apace . . ."

Kristen, watching, didn't really know that those adults rediscovering childhood through the benefice of Sonia's imagination included several regionally renowned writers and teachers, a classical concert guitarist, a prize-winning poet, a senator, two members of the state legislature, and the developer of a new drug rehabilitation program.

It didn't really matter—it was just fun to watch and Kristen smiled; it was nice too to hear the guitar music from the barn during the dancing, and last of all the quiet talk by the fireplace below Kristen's bedroom, as she fell asleep in this storybook house, on this warm summer night in 1969.

But that had been two summers ago, three treasure hunts ago, two harvests and growing seasons ago, and it was winter now, and the house was just barely to be seen through the falling snow, as the four adults talked quietly by the smaller fireplace of the field house. The snow was

covering over the memories of that treasure hunt and all
the treasure hunts and hikes and rides and picnics and so
many other gatherings, as though trying to cover
secrets. . . .

Brian continued to analyze the television interview,
wondered out loud why they—he and Sonia—had been
asked to appear, but knew the answer. If they had proved
an inspiration to their campus, they were no less so in this
community, to all who knew them. One grizzled old divorced landowner, Henrick, who had given them the first
of their three foals, had once, shyly, blushingly, told Sonia
and Brian, "Well, I hate marriage, the very idea. But you
know you two make it work so well for you. Who knows, I'll
keep an eye on you, and maybe someday I'll find out how to
make it work for me."

Brian had said there were rhythms to Sonia's movements around that grand house; she sent out significant
vibrations in her professional world as well. She was innovative, quickly showed herself to be a leader. She could
design programs, then gather and inspire the volunteers to
implement them. So wise for her to have switched from
botany to counseling when she met Brian; she had wanted
merely to be close to his field, but discovered it to be her
true metier as well.

Not the least lacking in humanitarian impulses, she
was yet a true social scientist, not just an unfocused ener-
getic driver nor naively optimistic do-gooder. In her
casework, she acted as both catalyst and chemical, relating
as a friend yet reacting as a counselor. She knew how to
help people examine and question the principles on which
their lives were based, inspired confidence through
troublesome transitional periods of growth. Though Brian,

afternoons at home while the children napped, wrote about counseling for professional journals, it was Sonia's theories and how she used them that he wrote of.

It was she who made people happier.

She had made Brian happier. She was more naturally at ease with people than he, but she helped him learn how to be attentive, how to share, how to learn *from*, give *to*. He had always been particularly shy around women, so she often had her close women friends over, to become his friends as well. Laura and Nadine, Melanie—and Elaine.

"At the end of the show we made the point, of course," Brian continued, "that this wasn't just an experiment with an expiration date. Sonia isn't just dabbling in her career. It's meaningful to her, and she has the freedom to grow in it as much as she can. If that means I become a more permanent 'house husband' than we'd originally intended, then that's the way it's got to be."

She had given him growth, he gave her scope and freedom to grow further.

"Did they bring it up, about your sex life?" Joe was caressing Elaine's hair but staring at Sonia.

"They asked us what we thought of infidelity. We corrected the vocabulary concept right away, explained that it was infidelity only if entered into furtively, so that it could cheat the other partner, cause him to cease knowing his mate, and thus be victimized. . . . We went into the 'comarital sexuality' concept and how that can open up one more field of human experience for additional richness and growth."

"But—"

"Oh, what they wanted to know about of course was us, but we just answered the question in general terms."

Brian and Sonia had opened themselves to "comarital

sexuality" at the end of their fifth year of marriage, after Dan was born. This was to be their last child, and seemed to represent some final act of commitment or concession to tradition. They had done it now—they'd done it all. All they had been trained and raised for. Education, Marriage, Work, Home, Parenthood.

They discussed their life a lot that year, examining it, not quite trusting its seeming perfection. No doubt they weren't the only young couple who, in 1968, the year the experts began to warn us of the death of marriage, looked around and wondered what they'd done.

Having got to this plateau, the American Dream of home, family, and material comforts, they restlessly asked themselves if there were not some peak beyond. *Was this all?* Comfortable as their life was, *was this all?* Personal growth would continue to lead them somewhere further, wouldn't it? The present always had to presage a somewhat different future, didn't it? If not, then what use in continuing and what point in even having come this far?

Further, certain aspects of their married life did not mesh perfectly. Sonia had more energy than Brian, lustier tastes in leisure-time activities. She would sometimes rise at dawn to ride over the misty hills for hours before breakfast, while he slept. She loved skiing, boating, tennis; he preferred films and seminars and lectures.

Not wanting to miss anything, sensing the richness of potential experience around them, they cast off, one by one, the restrictions and conventions of traditional marriage. A courtly and humane generosity was theirs, whereas most marriages were hallmarked by insecure possessiveness; most husbands and wives said to one another, *"I* don't want to go there! *We'll* stay home!" Sonia and Brian saw it differently:

"I'm not up for skiing, but you go," or "You go try silversmithing, I'll sign up for 'Realism in Films,' and we'll tell each other about the classes afterward." Even, "You go diving in Nassau for a week if you like, I'll see to the children; then when you get back, I'll go to give my paper at the Groves Conference."

They called this arrangement *independent intimacy*.

They called this lifestyle *Separate but Sharing*.

But unsurprisingly it sometimes happened that while they shared recollections of where they'd been with one another afterward, they shared the experience itself with other people.

There had been a time when Sonia and Joe had gone night skiing, returning afterward flushed and invigorated, laughing and sharing some private joke, and Joe had kissed Sonia warmly at the door as he waved good night to Brian.

"How was the skiing?" Brian asked.

"Wonderful. The snow was deep powder, I only fell once, and the high-lift operator knows your sister's friend Judy from when he used to work in Vail. . . ."

"I want to talk about this thing, Sonia."

"What? The skiing?"

"No. About the fact that Joe is getting to be very attracted to you."

Sonia shook the snow off her hat and jacket, hung them up.

Are the children asleep?

Yes.

All right then, Brian. Let's talk about it.

Two professional counselors sat down and faced each other, not at all sure of who was doctor, who was patient, sensing only that here was a need for preventive psychic medicine to be practiced.

Fact, said Sonia. *Joe is attracted to me.*

Premise, she continued. *Our marriage, yours and mine, is not a Hollywood, vine-covered type. We are not living a myth, you and I. Ours is a* real *marriage, it's organic, it grows and changes like those new sycamores out there, and we accept the opportunity for individual interchange with the society around us, to give regeneration and freshness to each and both of us. Agreed?*

Agreed, said Brian.

The depth of our love, it seems to me, can continually match the height of our humanity, our human experiences with others. We don't want the old habit pattern of pretending that we own each other, we want a new pattern of development somehow. Is that right?

Correct, said Brian.

Suppose then that at some time either of us wants to make love with someone else. Is sex to be set apart, prohibited, an area in which we are not free to seek experience and development? And I am not necessarily talking about Joe, Brian, because I am not necessarily attracted to him. I am talking about a basic underlying principle.

Sex outside of marriage complicates marriage, said Brian.

Now my goodness, Brian, just how would we know?

I'm speaking on the basis of clinical experience.

A clinical sample *brings in individuals who haven't fit their behavior into a workable frame of principles. They've slid into destructive behaviors of many kinds because they haven't known themselves.*

All right, I accept that. But I'd never want to do anything that might hurt you, and I would like to presume you feel the same. From your *experience then have you known anyone whose affairs outside of marriage have been free of negative consequences?*

This first thing you said is important, Brian. Hurting

each other, or anybody else, is absolutely wrong. We have to be sure that doesn't happen. But you could hurt me only by having a secret affair. If you had an affair and I knew about it that would mean you trusted me, the basic bond between us would still be central—and that's what counts. . . . And personally, no, I haven't known anyone who's had affairs outside of marriage without tragedy—I haven't known anyone, other than those I counsel, who've had affairs at all that I know of, but that doesn't mean it can't be handled. You and I are not like a lot of other people. I don't know a lot of people who can ride and ski without breaking legs and ankles, but we do.

You do. Bad analogy. The one time I went skiing I did break a knee. . . .

Sonia laughed. Well, sex is an indoor sport. . . .

Sport? We're talking about infidelity!

Definition of terms, said Sonia. We're not talking about faithlessness if we're looking at things honestly and looking for ways to enrich ourselves, individually and together, with no furtive, hidden, cheating quality. . . . It's not infidelity. It's something else. It's agreed-on extramarital sexuality, or comarital intimacy . . . and I can't believe you're not at least slightly interested in the chance, just the possibility, of making love to another woman, some woman, sometime, somewhere. After all, I'm the only woman you've ever slept with.

There's no one that I can think of.

Does it get down to that, Brian? You think that I have a partner in mind, and you don't? Or that I could find a partner and you couldn't?

Well . . . well, look, it's worked that way somewhat. I don't even go out for an evening for any purpose unless I know you have something to do; but you very often go off and leave me unoccupied, and if you ever went out for an evening with someone else and sex were to be involved, I really would be very hurt.

You're very fond of Elaine.

I'm very tolerant *of Elaine. I find Elaine dull.*

You don't give Elaine a chance, Brian. You intimidate her. Whenever she's around you use professional jargon, big words: she feels left out and self-conscious. You haven't made any effort at all to get to know her as often as she's been here, and I think she's *made a lot of overtures to try to know you. She's just more subtle than I am, that's all, and you're used to me.*

That's it. I'm used to you.

Well, I certainly don't want to change that. *Truly, Brian, I love you, we love each other, we are each other's orbit. That's central, that comes before anything else.* . . .

As long as it could be understood . . .

Yes?

That the marriage is central *and anything else is supplementary merely* . . .

That *is the whole idea.* A pause, Then, quietly:

Have we decided anything?

Brian, if it's all right with you, let's decide to keep the possibility–the possibility, mind you–open. . . .

Brian nodded slowly. *All right*, he said. *All right.* . . . *But of course*, he added, *don't you know that Elaine would be appalled at this conversation?*

No such thing, said Sonia. *You see, you* don't *know her. She has no more use, in principle, for monogamy than I have for astrology. I know, we've talked about it, she and I* . . .

Oh, said Brian. *Oh, I see.*

The principle established, only the occasion was

necessary; and it didn't come right away, but it did come—and what had been a close relationship among four people became an intimate arrangement, with Brian and Joe and Elaine discovering (to their infinite and deep relief) that you *could* continue to love your wife or husband while delighting in sexual involvement with another partner. Sonia, of course, had suspected this all along.

Happy to the point of being smug, yet tactful and mindful of the community and children, the four agreed that once a month ("more or less") the children would be taken to the grandparents or a neighbor and Sonia would carefully call some plan into play. There were several arrangements:

> *Plan A.* All four would go on a weekend trip somewhere, with two separate hotel rooms—one for Brian and Elaine, the other to be used by Joe and Sonia. Children to a neighbor.
>
> *Plan B.* One couple would go away, the other remained behind at the house. Children to grandparents.
>
> *Plan C.* Both couples remained at the house. (In this case the children could remain at home as well.)
>
> *Plan D.* Elaine would drive her car to Brian and Sonia's, Sonia would return to Joe and Elaine's, *in Elaine's car*, thus leaving correct cars in correct driveways. Children away.

Who could have called such an arrangement careless or rash; who could have claimed these couples to be impulsive or irresponsible? This was all planned so no one could possibly be hurt or victimized. This was all *very* well planned.

Brian got up, tiring of talking about the television show, to get more logs for the fire. "Somebody make coffee," he suggested as he went out into the snow. It seemed a good idea.

The temperature was edging downward, the snow was falling harder, but that would mean good sledding with the children tomorrow. And the following day it would be Christmas.

It was 1972.

This year, for the first time, Sonia had not planned a large holiday party for Christmas Eve. This year the four adults and two children were of themselves a close and loving unit, complete unto themselves—no outsiders necessary, except for old Henrick, who might drop by in the late afternoon. . . .

On Christmas Eve, Joe and Elaine arrived at the house early, to drink champagne touched with pear brandy, to laugh and talk, to trim a large tree Brian had brought in, and prepare the house for Christmas morning with surprises for the children.

Around midnight, each couple gave to the other what they believed to be an absolutely appropriate gift—a copy of *Open Marriage.* The gift card on Brian and Sonia's copy read, "To Two Who Could Have Written It"; and on the flyleaf of Joe and Elaine's copy Sonia had playfully written, "Stuff and Nonsense!"

And around midnight, Sonia brought out four very small identical boxes, her gifts for all four lovers—four identical rings, each of which she'd made from four slender bands of silver. Two bands were united in the center, framed by two other bands slightly separated from the double band, on either side. Who did the two center bands represent, asked Brian. Only Elaine guessed: they represented her and Sonia, for it was their total, trusting, open friendship which had brought them all together.

And in the morning, Sonia would fix a hearty Christmas breakfast, while Dan would thunder downstairs announcing, "I'm going to get presents cause I've been *good*," with Kristen close behind adding, "And *I'm* going to get presents because I'm *adorable*," then climb up on Aunt Ellie's lap to hear stories from *The Animal Book*. . . .

It was 1972.

And it was still perfect then, and Elaine was still Aunt Ellie then, and the couples were seeing each other intimately only every two weeks ("more or less") and the neighbors were still either polite and liberated or dense and imperceptive.

The trouble would come later.

Later that year, Plan D would become a weekly occurrence, then an almost nightly one. Sonia would feel herself sliding from control as "camp counselor," coordinator of all the intimate plans and schedules: The initiative would come from others. The children would begin to be innocently curious, the neighbors nosy, certain few coworkers given to double entendres, lascivious innuendo, knowing sideways glances. . . .

Mr. Brady the miller would, two weeks in succession, find Elaine at the house while Sonia was at her job—and wonder. Kristen would one fatal evening astonish a small gathering of friends by asking Elaine brightly, loudly, *"Are you staying here with my daddy tonight?"*

Later that year, Joe would say accusingly to Elaine, "For Christ's sake can't you be home once in a while?" And on a weekend at Tanglewood Lodge (such foursome weekends rare now, Plan A almost inoperative) Sonia would say to Brian as they were dancing, "Hey, how would you like it if just for a change your own wife shared your room tonight?" and feel stabbed by his distant, disappointed look. . . .

And Joe would say to Sonia, "You can move in with me, you know; we do love each other after all," and Sonia would respond, angrily, uncompromising, "No, we *don't* love each other; you're only fooling yourself because you feel left out. . . ."

And Sonia would say to Brian, "Let's talk about this situation with Joe and Elaine," and Brian would respond, "Okay," and Sonia would say, "Joe is fun in bed, and we're fond of each other, and it's good, but I'd never prefer another man to you," and Brian would respond, obliquely, "Something about Elaine makes me feel protective toward her. . . ."

And Sonia would one afternoon walk into the house to find Brian and Elaine seated at the kitchen table, holding hands and looking at each other with utter absorption, each in the other; and Sonia would wonder who the two center bands on all those silver rings represented now. . . .

And Sonia and Joe would meet privately and plan to distract their mates with new activities, other people, so that the four of them would have no time to see each other "except as friends," and Sonia would buy a new soft pant-suit to wear around the house, and she would be seductive and solicitous toward Brian, but a response was just not there, was just not in him anymore. . . .

And Sonia would, later that year, notice that in a book of astrology poems Elaine had given to Brian for his birthday she had written, *"On the day of your birth my life began also. . . ."*

Later that year, the fairy tale would end, the "arrangement" would lose its structure, the game would lose its rules, and things would be out of control totally, and everyone would know that Elaine and Brian were in love.

And Joe would talk to Sonia about it. And Sonia would

talk to Brian. And Elaine would talk to Brian, and Joe to Elaine; but the four of them could not face it together, and when the four *were* together there was a tense pretended blindness, a stiff false gaiety. Myopia, and pain.

And Brian would try painfully to tell Sonia, "We gave each other freedom to grow, and we *did* grow, and we're deeper and richer now for it. But we grew in different ways. . . ."

And Elaine would say to Sonia, "I'm happier in a more traditional role than you are, and that's what Brian needs right now. He needs me, not you; and *I need him.*"

And Elaine and Brian would vow to give it up, to hurt themselves rather than the others, and never to see each other anymore. And then an hour later one of them would call the other.

But that would all come later.

Now, with another log put on the fire and the coffee made, Joe, who had been sitting with his arms around Elaine would come to embrace Sonia; and Elaine would move to Brian to take his coat, still murmuring some teasing comment about the apron, and he would hug her tenderly. And it seemed this cozy night could last forever among these four lovers, while the snow fell harder, as though trying to cover secrets (or seeds of secrets) with so much weight and chill that they could not spring forth and blossom with their awful knowledge when the season changed.

And no one could foresee, just then, the final week in June—the week when Joe and Sonia would know there was no choice, and tell each other, "We have to let them go, they have to have their chance."

No one could guess, that night, that Sonia would have to pack her things, and put away her saddles, and tell her children, "I'll always be your mother, and I'll always love you, but I have to go away. . . ." that Sonia would say to Brian and Elaine that she would always love them, too ("You were my best friend and will be always, I couldn't leave my family in better hands," to Elaine; and to Brian a simple whispered, *"Remember all the good things, remember all you can. . . ."*) before finally driving away in the aging green Griffith, down the winding driveway a little too fast in the fading summer light, skimming over the hills in the lane, sycamores blurring in the rear-view mirror, and wondering.

Wondering what these things called growth and freedom truly meant; and why it sometimes gets so difficult to apply philosophy and theory to human arrangements . . . wondering if some traditional areas of marriage should have been guarded zealously, some aspects of innovative patterns held under strict control; wondering whether, taken all in all, absolute freedom, just as surely as absolute submission, can destroy absolutely.

Emotional Freedom:

Love, Marriage, Commitment

> *The latter half of our century is comparatively poor in remarkable women. Now, when women are more exacting than they used to be, they are of less importance than of old. We have rows of women artists, women scientists, and authoresses . . . yet, with all that, they are of less importance than they used to be. The more that woman seeks to assert her influence by main force, the less her influence as an individual; the more she imbues this century with her spirit, the fewer her conquests as a woman. It is a peculiar sign of the times that, in spite of the many restrictions of former days, men and women have never understood each other more badly than now. . . . Each goes his or her own way; there may be a nervous search for each other and a short finding, but it is soon followed by a speedy losing.*[1]

Thus, in 1896, in the polite style of expression characteristic of her day, Laura Marholm-Hansson expressed the view that emancipation and accomplishment on the part of women proved divisive to relations between the sexes—and this in turn proved ultimately unsatisfactory to the women themselves.

She chose to illustrate her belief in her book, *Modern Women*, by describing the fate of several gifted women of international fame: the mathematician Sonia Kovalevsky, winner of the Prix Bordin on Christmas Eve in 1888, of whom it was said, "Science is her chief delight," but whom Hansson viewed as "an unhappy, injured little woman running through the woods with a wailing cry for her husband"; Eleonora Duse, who grew "tired, unspeakably tired" on continual tour and yearned for domesticity rather than the exercise of art; and others.

A generation later, radical feminist "Red Emma" Goldman surprised her comrades in the liberation movement of the early 1900s by echoing Hansson's concern—by speaking of "the emptiness and narrowness of the existing conception of woman's emancipation, and its tragic effect upon the inner life of woman." The higher the mental development of woman, she hypothesized, the less possible it is for her to meet a congenial mate who will see in her not only sex, but also a human being and friend.

Dramatically, she wrote of "the artificial stiffness and narrow respectabilities of women's liberation, which produce an emptiness in woman's soul that will not let her drink from the fountain of life."[2] (The "fountain of life" referred to a sustained relationship of warmth and love.)

A classic expression of the need to reject love was contained in early feminist Margaret Sanger's letter to her husband, in which she wrote that the achievement of her goal—*i.e.*, freedom of women to control their reproductive function—depended on the abandonment of every other; that their relationship of twelve years must end; that she could no longer be his wife, since she "belonged to the world."

In historical perspective, this is no pompous self-evaluation, but simple fact. Though Margaret Sanger's life after her separation touched on several relationships of intimacy or love, these were interludes only: She did not achieve (and perhaps did not seek to achieve) an enduring and total commitment to another man. Her crusade was too important; in fact, all-absorbing.

Contemporary examples crowd to mind. Many feminists have separated from husbands and families; others have scrupulously avoided marriage, or its equivalent, in the first place. Why? Does the language and philosophy of social reform seep inevitably into the area of private relationships, poisoning the "fountain of life" that Emma Goldman referred to? Does it turn personal relationships into political confrontations? Was the possibility considered that sisterhood, for some or many, would necessitate a solitary life? Plainly asked, does liberation preclude love?

If, only yesterday (before the Redstocking generals took over the *Tonight* show, and the troops of CR groups followed, taking over neighborhood church basements) love seemed a worthy goal, an unquestioned good . . . if, only yesterday, our thoughts were to be occupied with love sweet love, what is this thing called love, this one thing the world's got too little of . . . well, that *was* yesterday.

Now our very emotional vocabulary is undergoing siege and becoming regimented; and we're not to speak of love but instead employ terms such as "relating" or "interacting." Now contemporary feminist Lisa Hobbs is compelled to observe that "among my more radical sisters I am not counted a true feminist for I use the word *love* too often,"[3] and a California woman writes, "I'm going to have to give up falling in love and I'm not kidding; if fudge makes your face break out you either have to live with a pimply face or give up fudge; there's absolutely no point in arguing that other people manage to eat fudge with no ill effects,"[4] and no one less than Ti-Grace Atkinson states firmly that "Love will not survive the liberation of women."

Ah yes, here's the point where lots of us get very nervous. "Surely we can't change or do away with love, can we?" we ask; and the radical sector calmly answers, "But of course. Why not?"

Why not indeed? Increasingly, after all, we live in a technological environment, a scientific age which has no room for mystery and ambiguity: Science murders myth. We hear much less about Prometheus since we learned the scientific facts of lightning; and we profess less need for love since Germaine Greer.

Even before Greer and Atkinson, some perceived that love was doing a totally inadequate job of meeting our needs. In fact, love seemed called upon to fill new needs—needs unknown, no doubt, in pretechnological societies, when love (and the leisure necessary to recognize it) were quite different matters. One somehow imagines that men and women didn't worry quite so much about emotional fulfillment in the Stone Age, when control of one's immediate environment required total attention if one was to survive.

But many men and women in this century have given up attempts to control the environment we live in, the world around us. (What use? What can one do about famine, fallout, global cooling, continental drift, the fact that India has the bomb and Iran the oil? Not a damned thing. Pull in the periscopes of personal concern, then, and direct our thoughts within a narrowed, homier sphere.) What matters, after all, is *people*, and if only we can find answers in the people around us, and make them understand and *love* us, then we will matter, too.

After World War II, as feelings of panic and futility about the human situation and global future grew, so in direct proportion developed the cult of Personal Adjustment, the mania for Personal Acceptance, the fascination with communicating, relating, understanding. . . .

With awesome seriousness we tried to figure one another out, to break each other's codes. Parents learned *childrenese*, and consenting adults carried out private seminars in body language. *Communication* was the most prominent personal hobby around, in addition to being the latest means of mass information-sharing. "I'm really getting into knowing others," people said to one another; "More than anything, it's important to communicate," registrants told one another, murmuring at first, as shy as winter swimmers, at weekend encounter marathons. Communication was the major preoccupation of the day; but of course what we didn't say because we were too "modern" was that we were really after love, for which communication was just the current synonym.

But this search for communication, mutual knowledge—love—which until recently the sexes held as common goal, seemed to arouse quite different needs and fears in men and women. Men feared losing their personhood when they loved, women feared not finding theirs.

And feminists who today have managed to attain that sort of validation or self-worth (say, in work) that males have generally had, tend to adopt the characteristic male habit of pulling out of love affairs at crucial moments, in an abrupt impulsive gesture which they believe to be a movement of self-preservation, never to return to that illogical state quite so deeply as before, frightened off by something ill-defined but threatening. (One more example, it seems, of how feminists accept and imitate male patterns.)

The spectre which seems to threaten is the idea of dependence, for too often and too easily dependence becomes subservience and subordination, lending more than a little truth, perhaps, to Firestone's complaints of "the destructive guise of love," her contention that "Male culture was built on the love of women, and at their expense."[5]

Male exploitation of female love is indeed galling to any woman who aspires to autonomy, for this problem can't be easily resolved or remedied or even analyzed. It doesn't come neatly packaged, ready for an action program: There are handy statistics available concerning the number of women who suffer physical assault, credit discrimination, or inequity of pay, but no statistics have yet been gathered to indicate the number of women victimized by their own emotions,* and the rights and respects due women in love are nowhere mentioned in the ERA.

But if love's potential damage can't be tempered in the crucible of law, then some control may still be hoped for if it can be crucified by rhetoric: thus, to Carolyn Jones and Judith Brown, "Love is at best an inadequate reward for women's bizarre heritage of oppression";[7] to Carolyn Bird, "Romantic love is a putup job utilized to trap women into giving up their identities";[8] to Kate Millett, "Romantic love affords a means of emotional manipulation which the male is free to exploit";[9] and in Ti-Grace Atkinson's summation of a long and thoughtful analysis, "Love is the psychological pivot in the persecution of women."

Atkinson has more to say on the subject. Love is unacceptable because "it can be felt by one party only; it is unilateral by nature and is thus rendered contradictory and irrational." It is "woman's pitiful deluded attempt to attain the human, by fusing with the powerful." It is "anxiety converted into functional symptoms of illness."[10]

*Firestone, however, estimates that "For every successful contemporary love experience, for every short period of enrichment, there are ten *de*structive love experiences, post-love "downs" of much longer duration.[6]

Romance must go too since it consists of our personal symbolism for male-female love, and the symbol is as tainted as the reality it represents: "Romance is the opiate of oppressed women," the drug which can prevent women from even recognizing that they are ill, and that love is the disease from which they suffer.

And marriage? The moderates among the feminists approach the concept of marriage with mere healthy caution and skepticism, the radicals with lusty rage. The moderates are content to warn of inequities, to advise guarding against exploitation with contracts; to warn of the difficulty of reconciling the *stability* of marriage with the growth and change and complexity necessary for an emerging feminist identity, to counsel a married woman to make sure the overriding principle of her life remains *I*, not *we*.

The radicals, however, are serious about the abolition of the institution. "Traditional marriage is destined for the fire," states Hobbs simply.

"Marriage is a form of slavery," says Sheila Cronan. [And] "since marriage constitutes slavery for women, it is clear that the Women's Movement must concentrate on attacking this institution. Freedom for women cannot be won without the abolition of marriage."[11] Or again, "We women can use marriage as the 'dictatorship of the proletariat' in the family revolution. When male supremacy is completely eliminated, marriage, like the state, will wither away."[12]

The radical feminist organization founded by Atkinson and known simply as The Feminists declared in their organizational charter:

> Because The Feminists considers the institution of marriage inherently inequitable in both its formal (legal) and informal (social) aspects; because we consider this in-

stitution a primary formalization of the persecution of women; because we consider rejection of this institution both in theory and practice necessary for extensive and independent work in feminism; because we consider the destruction of marriage *by women* an essential part of our progress toward liberation; we establish a membership quota; that no more than one-third of our members can be participants in either a formal (with legal contract) or informal (living with a man) instance of the institution of marriage.[13]

Finally, *Toward A Female Liberation Movement* advised serious feminists to be prepared to end their marriages:

Those radical females already married should be prepared to make a decision about how they will live their lives in order to have time for their political activities. If you plan to live with your husband, you will have to begin making changes in the marital pattern. And the chances are that unless he has a radical analysis which is pretty thorough, your marriage will end in divorce.

This same publication defines marriage as

a relationship which is oppressive politically, exhausting physically, stereotyped emotionally and sexually, and atrophying intellectually. (A woman teams up with an individual groomed from birth to rule, and she is equipped for revolt only with the foot-shuffling, head-scratching gestures of "feminine guile.")

They continue,

Some women will have to remove themselves totally from the marriage arrangement which insists that they love, in a predetermined style, their own personal masters. And married women will have to remove themselves periodically to revitalize their commitment to their sex and to the liberation movement.[14]

Or, if marriage exists, it should have an episodic quality (the Jones/Brown dictum summons up visions of women
scheduling recurrent retreats from their homes); or it
should be contractual; and it should ideally be open sexually, to avoid possessiveness and stifling interdependen-
cies.

The concept of open marriage is another scale-tipping
act in the name of equality and justice between the sexes.
In most societies, men have traditionally been allowed sexual prerogatives outside marriage, but women have not.
The blatant injustice of this social code could be coped with
by requiring husbands to stay home or allowing wives to
stray; and the former being patently unenforceable, and
the latter being in tune with the times and the newly adventurous spirit of liberated women, the choice was clear.
The confining principle of monogamy (wherein grasping
was common and giving was rare) was to be replaced by an
attitude of openness that came close, at times, to resem-
bling indifference. John and Mimi Lobell, the exemplary,
openly married couple chosen by New York NOW Sexuality Committee to represent this live style at NOW Sexuality Conferences, have had about twenty lovers over the
past four years, counting not only semipermanent liaisons
but one-night stands, with no discernible problems: Mimi,
in fact, in an interview, fondly recalled her husband's first
fling, which took place at their home: "I found myself becoming a good hostess," she laughed. Her own sexual experiences outside of marriage came close to becoming love
affairs once or twice (particulary with students who had
"romantic hang-ups"). Both husband and wife spoke disap-
provingly of such involvement; the Lobells hold it as a firm
principle that open marriage works best when you do not
fall in love with other people.[15]

But approved models of relationships for the future may be so open that they may not be based on man-woman "pair-bonding" at all.

Shulamith Firestone envisions alternatives such as

> a loose social form in which two or more partners, of whatever sex, enter a nonlegal/sex/companionate arrangement the direction of which varies with the internal dynamics of the relationship. . . . After several generations of nonfamily living, our psychosexual structures may become altered so radically that the monogamous couple, or the "aim-inhibited" relationship, would become obsolescent. We can only guess what might replace it—perhaps true "group marriages," transsexual group marriages which also involved older children? We don't know . . .

However, she continues,

> We want to *broaden* these options to include many more people for longer periods of their lives, to transfer here all the cultural incentives now supporting marriage —making these alternatives, finally, as common and acceptable as marriage is today.[16]

There are a lot of attempted separations pointed to by such models: Built into the attempt to separate sexual exclusivity from marriage is an implicit separation of romantic love from marriage—and, if only as a matter of convenience, love from extramarital or nonmarital relationships.

Underlying the attempts to make these separations —these neat, clean breaks—seems a compulsion to excise troublesome emotional behavior from the nature of the female, leaving her freer (as the male has supposedly been) to work, create, and grow, unhampered by strictures of sexual loyalty and possessiveness.

To some, this challenge to "de-nature" came as a surprise; but perhaps it shouldn't have been so surprising. When the talk is of equality, after all, the discussion can quickly range from equal pay to equal play. . . . and if feminists are serious about equality with men, then one obvious avenue would be to emulate men's supposed relative independence from debilitating emotions.

And much of what this society characterizes as typical or desirable "feminine" emotional patterns might well be rejected, for much of what this society calls femininity consists of a trait that is common in small children: dependency—a looking up to someone larger and more powerful with a gaze in the eyes that says "Feed me," "I need my shoes tied," or "I'm helpless."

Perhaps the quality of the "feminine" that is being castigated by radical feminists is *dependency*, not love itself; *dependency*, not romantic accouterments; *dependency in marriage*, not marriage itself.

For insofar as society defines the feminine as the "childlike" or the "helpless," the concept does indeed need to be rejected. Indeed, it's possible that society even views children with more potential for growth and autonomy, for we share the pride of the growing child in his or her developing abilities ("I can do it myself now"), yet we set limits to the degree in which women are to grow and develop. Grown women are expected to tie their own shoes, but are supposed to be unable to open doors or hail taxis if a man is available to do these things on their behalf. Women internalize a certain amount of this (believing we're not "supposed" to be able to hail taxis, we actually find we're not too good at it), and while this is relatively harmless as long as the woman recognizes the game she's playing —distinguishes role-playing from reality—there's also a loss of dignity.

And other dependencies—emotional ones that have little to do with the business of opening doors—linger with more virulence due to society's view of woman-as-child.

Women have been raised to need, from men, approval, sustenance, love, support, and even reinforcement of their own opinions. And most women retain some vestige of this need if they continue to socialize with men: Whether we are traditionally feminine women or moderately consciousness-raised women or radical feminist separatists, virtually all of us change our behavior to some extent when men walk into the room (if only to become more guarded and defensive so our need won't show).

The dependency needs women retain, though, ought to differ from those of children, insofar as they should be based on a sense of self, a "center" as the feminists would have it; and should be subject to control. Out of control, they become neuroses, and women become victims.

Two examples, widely varying, might be given:

K., a woman whose husband wished to leave her, confessed her terror at the prospect to a friend, Betty. K. recalled tearfully that she had begged him, "Please stay. I accept that you don't love me. You needn't touch me or even talk to me. Just *be here*."

"How sad," Betty said, discussing K., "to so completely lack self-worth." Betty perceived K.'s problem as one of "neurotic, parasitic, eviscerating dependence," projecting as she spoke a calm, serene picture of her *own* autonomy. Betty had been through consciousness raising, and was in fact a CR facilitator, and seemed to have a clear view of intersex "dependency traps" and to be quite immune to them. I told her, "I have a friend, Arthur, whose only experience seems to be with women who are clinging and dependent. I've tried to tell him that not all women are that way. I'd like for him to meet you." Betty said that would be all right. They went out once, twice, each informing me matter-of-factly that they were quite pleased to have met the other. Then they slept together. Betty called me the next morning to say that she was struggling with "an annoying regression," and called Arthur that afternoon to tell him "I can't live without you."

Many women can talk a good game of independence—as long as they're not tested, as long as men are nowhere in their social world. And most of us, in most ways, are fortunate enough to go through life not being tested as to whether the principles we profess are truly held. We can say we'd never push another person off a lifeboat to save ourselves, plant a hidden microphone to feed a vaulting ambition, or award a contract based on an enticing stock option, and we will never know whether these things are true or not; we can claim not to be addicted to material comforts as we sit in a well-appointed apartment, fed and clothed and warm.

But it's not easy to protect ourselves from tests of any theories we claim relevant to men and women. And perhaps we'd do better (we women of this generation, anyway) to acknowledge our lingering dependencies, and work to control them rather than deny them.

A controlled degree of retained dependency can easily be distinguished from the neurotic degree, and the criterion is simple: a normal need can be met, a neurotic need cannot. (It is compulsive, insatiable.) A woman with only normal dependency needs can sustain herself during those periods of time when emotional support is not available; and when it is available, she will respond with growth. A woman with neurotic dependencies calls upon men constantly to gratify emotional demands; yet regardless of how much support is given, she does not grow. She, like K. (and like Betty) has a degree of dependency that might almost be termed an addiction—*not* a metaphorical addiction, but a real one. Like K., deprived of a familiar man, she might show "withdrawal symptoms"; or, like Betty, she might be able to remain "sober" only if she keeps her distance from the source of her addiction (much like an alcoholic who dares not touch even one glass of wine or liquor). In such extremes, one can begin to understand the radical feminists' designation of love or romance as "opiates."

To meet this problem, many liberated women attempt another "separation"—sex from love. This one is happening all over. A woman friend of mine who is an artist discussed her sex life candidly: "Everyone who knows me thinks I'm terribly dedicated to my work, and celibate, because I never go out," Irene explains, "but the truth is I have men over all the time. This week there's Jerry, who takes late lunch hours so he doesn't conflict with Mike, who comes in early. Then there's Greg . . ." By the time she finished talking, she seemed to have named half a dozen names. I asked her to tell me something more about these men, what their jobs were, what they were like. She looked surprised at the question. "What are they *like*? My dear, except for penis size, and frequency and duration, of course, I haven't the vaguest idea. That's the entire point, you know. You shouldn't get to know them. . . ."

Actually, in an article entitled "Casualties of the Sex War," feminist Karen Durbin reacts to such situations with some concern. She writes:

> A friend of mine reports that the women he meets are becoming increasingly alarming. He describes a typical evening; he's asked his agent's assistant out for a drink. Afterward, they stop at her apartment. He kisses her once or twice. ("It seemed expected of me," he said.)

She immediately began to take her clothes off. "Wait a minute," he said, "I don't even know you." "That's all right," she replied. "I prefer to fuck men I don't know. It's better that way."[17]

Better that way? Better in what way? And for whom? And for what reasons? And for how long? Reflecting on such couplings, one recalls a famous story of a psychiatrist who ushered guests into his living room one day, quite unperturbed by the fact that his eight-year-old daughter and a boy neighbor of similar age were engaged on the sofa in what closely resembled an act of sexual intercourse. "Do you think it's a good idea to permit them such activity so early?" asked an astonished visitor. "It does no harm," came the psychiatrist's calm reply. "It's only a game to them now of course. When they get older they'll invest it with what meaning they will. But it does the young no harm to play games."

Perhaps it does the young no harm. But even presuming so it might be natural to view passing relationships with constantly changing partners (sex-as-game) as a transitory phase only, characteristic of a youthful phase of emotional development only, and that "whatever meaning" of sexuality might evolve with emotional adulthood there *would* be *some meaning.*

It seems a paradox that the emancipated woman, long tired of being regarded by men as a sex object, nonetheless makes both of herself and her partner just such an object by rejecting the emotional involvements that accompany sex. What is sex without emotion, without love? It is touching, stroking, holding, fingering, embracing, thrusting, responding. And that's all it is. It is *not* caring, accepting, affirming, needing, committing, appealing, knowing, giving, or *risking.*

Maybe it's "better that way" because there *is* no risk, and when sex and love do occur together, as we were told they should, there is a risk (the risk that the love will turn out to be "unilateral in nature . . . therefore irrational" as Atkinson suggests). And for those who started mixing sex and love before Atkinson was around to point out the irrationality of that indulgence, there were occasional—even embittering—surprises, to be sure.

"I didn't realize," one woman wrote, "that love could reverse itself, could be withdrawn, or that the consequence of such a withdrawal could be so powerful as to crush vast expanses of one's own potential for feeling. I didn't realize there actually was such a thing as falling apart over the loss of love. . . ."[18] Expressed as a simple principle then: Sex with strangers is better, because after all one needn't fall apart if a near-total stranger never comes back.

Still, perhaps the "emancipation" that's being evidenced here is merely either a casting off of inhibitions—or a different kind of capitulation to sexism. True emancipation should mean freedom to achieve *new* values for both sexes, not just for the female to discard the old "feminine" frame of reference and adopt the stereotyped "masculine" one.

Alex Berkman, writing of the so-called sexually emancipated women of another generation, in a letter to Emma Goldman speculated that this "is just a kind of superficial sexuality without rhyme or reason. . . . At the bottom of it is an inner emptiness, sexual and otherwise. They hunger for a real affection, which they do not get; they only get sex. And one of the reasons they do not get it, is because the thing has become both cause and effect. Need of affection is the cause of their behavior, and their behavior becomes the cause why they cannot get real affection, nor feel it after a while. . . .

"Well, it is their affair," Berkman concluded.[19]

Or is it?

Now, sex without love is no capital crime. But neither is it socially cohesive or personally affirming. For all that it may offer in terms of temporary libidinous satisfaction, release of tension, or diversion from loneliness, the paradigm of "If we're liberated, we'll have sex; but since we're liberated, who needs love?" is not only sexual nihilism if it is the principle of constant motivation, but is in a sense its own kind of capitulation to sexism by emulating what has been typically regarded as "masculine" behavior.

And radical feminists seem at times to convert loveless sex from an expression of nihilism to a symptom of outright hostility: *loveless sex may in fact be the attempt of radical women to simultaneously define men as the enemy, and yet consort with the enemy—by doing so in an uncaring, mutually exploitative way.*

But if one sleeps with men, and if men are the enemy, then does not sex become a war game? Can we not expect a few casualties of spirit (perhaps even as Berkman suggested, an *inability to care* deeply or spiritually, after a while)?

Is there any answer for those who are wary of open marriage or the futuristic models proposed by Firestone, for those women who would like to enjoy some ongoing commitment with a man, rather than the "short finding and speedy losing" that characterizes so many autonomous (but essentially emotionless) encounters.

One might, for a start, return to Atkinson's definition of love, "the pitiful deluded attempt of women to attain the human by fusing with the powerful," and find a clue to separating love from dependence in the word *power*. If one brings one's own power to a relationship, one need not depend on power and/or protection shed by another. But neither can one substitute the power only.

It's essential to realize, too, that dependency can't be separated out of love, leaving pure element for adulterated compound: dependency is—must be—part of love, for in love someone *matters* to you, and therefore your well-being is not to be determined by you alone.

And any attempt to remove the element of dependency—and thus to implicitly treat love as a cognitive act only, with measured mutuality of emotions, is doomed. Any effort to impose a conscious power principle on love—to treat love as a cognitive art—is as unworkable as, say, an effort to make a timepiece of a magnet, a statue of a shadow, an essay of a sonnet, or impose *Robert's Rules of Order* on storms and sunlight: the very imposition of the form destroys the essence.

Emotions simply can't be structured or scheduled for "rational" human purposes: Forces of the past (whether inchoate memories of tenderness we knew as children, as Freud would have it, or the archaic echoes of a collective unconscious, as described by Jung) cannot simply be reasoned away. To some extent—whatever the precise nature of the past forces that have created our present relationships—who we love is beyond our control. Those relationships which may seem the least logical may yet prove the most deeply compelling. The total inner record of our past life creates a rich and unique *gestalt* at any given time, within each of us, embodying that potential for risk-taking, for giving and caring which finds expression in the emotion we term *love*.

But if the mode of expression must fit within a conscious frame of rightness or logical priorities, one gets only the rightness and not the richness: One is left with the timepiece, essay, or rule book only—not the shadows and the sonnets, the storms and sunlight.

Of course the feminist theorists sense this, and do not attempt to impose logic on love, but rather to replace love with logic. This is why they do not write of love so often as of logic, or respect, or egalitarianism; of fulfillment, of the exploration of potential; of deals and bargains, of contracts, of balanced emotional investments and returns that are to occur within businesslike, nondependent relationships.

Granted, this is safer, more enforceable. *Love, honor and obey* is impractically, astrally vague. Replace it with "Wife strips beds, husband remakes them; wife cooks meals on weekends, husband picks up laundry and dry cleaning on alternate Thursdays." One thus approaches the institutionalized form of male-female love much like a wary consumer approaches a marketplace where the incautious will be robbed or cheated.

Perhaps wariness *is* in order; perhaps there *have* been victimizations; perhaps sometimes inferior goods *are* foisted on an unsuspecting bargainer. But perhaps one might also ask the quality of the coin with which the bargain is being made.

Love seems to exact too high a cost only if "purchased" by someone who is impoverished in other areas of personal development; only if it is sought exclusive of other avenues of communication, interest, and self-expression; only if one's thoughts and energies are tied too closely to those of the person who is loved.

But giving up altogether on the phenomenon and the commitment it implies seems to be an unsatisfactory resolution: I've seen precious little evidence that total emotional independence offers women happier lives than controlled dependencies in love. And though a woman who retains some dependencies (is unafraid to lean, if not to cling) and admits wanting and weakness on occasion, certainly risks having her weaknesses scorned or her wants unmet at times, she's not apt to go through many days screaming—or stifling screams (and she is further retaining behavior that could serve as a desirable model for men in this transitional time—for if women have been encouraged to nurture their dependencies, men have been trained to stifle theirs) for she's not attempting to isolate herself from a network of human bonds which can be the basis of growth as well as of occasional pain. Whereas the woman who aims for total independence will find an arid situation of total isolation that is ultimately dehumanizing: If no man is an island, no woman can be either—not even a radical feminist.

Sammie:

"Men Belong in Their

Own Universe"

Large rooms, bare floors. Toys everywhere. Broken toys, faded toys, shells of toys—the flotsam carelessly washed up by the tides of two childhoods, now being picked over by another child, a little girl of four.

A doll, pretty and whole when older sister June was little, now wears a dingy white cutoff sock rather than its former pretty satin dress. The doll's eyes were taken out by older sister June last year: An article said that dolls' eyes were often affixed by dangerous pins—June feared for the safety of the smaller child. The eyes as it turned out were glued in, not pinned, but they've gotten lost in any case, and the doll now stares unseeingly at the fragile little girl now crooning to it. . . . the little girl seems not to mind.

A plastic dial telephone once belonging to an older brother will be played with next; it's broken too, the cord connecting the receiver severed. The little girl dials seven digits, counting carefully, then runs around the room, detached receiver to her ear, chatting expectantly, "Hello, hello . . . " No answer. No matter.

On the wall, a photo of the little girl, whose name is Gwen (just between the *Fuck Housework* and *Wonder Woman for President* posters). The photo was taken on Gwen's third birthday, when she took part in her first radical feminist demonstration, protesting the distribution of an objectionable IUD. A black-and-white Polaroid photo shows her small, tousled, curly head peeking from behind a large poster proclaiming, "I hope it will be safer to be a woman when I grow up."

These are the rooms where Sammie's children live. Sammie, of course, lives here too, or at least she sleeps here for three hours of the night and is almost always home for breakfast and dinner.

It works this way. At 6 A.M., before dawn touches this solid block of concrete-block apartment buildings in Mernonette Park, on Chicago's far South Side, Sammie is up—pulling off the sweatshirt she sleeps in and pulling on another one, gathering together her knapsack of paper work for the day, and cooking. Both breakfast and dinner are prepared at once. The pancake batter is mixed, the skillet heated, the oatmeal put in the double boiler, the orange juice poured, the coffee plugged in, the eggs boiled. Somehow, simultaneously, five frozen pork chops or hamburger patties are taken from the freezer (only five per meal, never any second helpings—food stamps modify the grocery budget problem but don't solve it), then put into a casserole dish with canned potatoes and frozen peas and carrots, and shoved into the oven. By five o'clock they'll thaw, and preteen June, home from school, will turn the oven on to heat the mixture for dinner.

Lettuce is washed and drained and put into a plastic bag, Jell-O put into molds and refrigerated. Finally, between setting the table and waking the children and timing the eggs and turning the pancakes, Sammie also makes a peanut butter and jelly sandwich for Gwen's lunch and puts the sandwich in a plastic bag. . . .

Breakfast.

"The kids are up at seven, and at the table by seven-fifteen. Breakfast lasts an hour. We all sit and talk. It's very together. It's very important. It's a symbolic meal, a sharing way of beginning the day as a family unit." Never any variation. Sammie never sleeps late.

The older children, June and Steve, leave for school at eight-fifteen, and the next few hours belong to little Gwenna. There are some interruptions: A colleague of Sammie's from the women's center needs to know "where it's at with the reform guidelines" (being drawn up for presentation to the local TV stations); a fledgling feminist who has just heard of Sammie calls to ask hesitant, searching, detailed questions about the Tuesday evening meetings; Sammie's new volunteer assistant, who calls every morning about ten to report on the morning's mail and phone calls, usually has a problem or two—the weekly dances aren't bringing in enough money to pay the rent, and contributions are off; or crazy Lee is going around to the more conservative women's organizations and scaring people; or the mayor's staff has postponed an appointment for the third time.

Just after eleven, mother and daughter are off for a bus ride to the baby sitter's (except on days when Sammie doesn't have the money for the sitter and must take Gwen to work with her); then Sammie is on another 111A bus, this time in the opposite direction, past her apartment building at the corner of Londale, all the way to the Dan Ryan train, changing at the Ninety-Fifth Street terminal for a local into Chicago's Loop, where she'll exit at the Wabash and Randolph stop, then walk one block to Michigan Avenue to catch a final bus, the 157 Sheridan Road, to within six blocks of her office. (Sammie's job, for which she's barely paid, is running Chicago's most radical feminist center). Late mornings, the "L" cars and buses aren't crowded, and Sammie can pull out some papers from her knapsack and work during the two twenty-minute "L" rides, scribbling lists of things to do: alphabetize the growing card file of lesbian feminist organizations; generate more mail to protest the NBC show "Flowers of Evil"; find out what Media Report to Women in Washington is all about; phone the Parks Department to ask about use of city buildings for meetings and dances; find out *who* it is in the mayor's office who's sabotaging efforts to discuss the equal-rights bill now before the city council; talk to Ann. . . .

It's not possible to work on the ride home at five o'clock (not even possible to sit down on the Sheridan Road bus, crowded with commuters), when Sammie will take the Dan Ryan trains back to the South Side, walk (or run) the blocks to the apartment for the dinner June has ready. (The buses are too crowded at that hour to even bother with; Sammie is mildly claustrophobic anyway). There's to be less time with the kids now than there was at breakfast, but "How was your day?" questions can be asked and answered before Sammie bestows 'bye-again kisses and hugs around the table, and dashes (or sprints) back to the "L" platform (unless a bus comes along at just the right time and it probably won't—service is irregular after 6 P.M.) in order to be back downtown by seven-fifteen for the Monday night coordinating committee meetings. Or the Tuesday night CR facilitators' meetings. Or the media meetings (Wednesdays), the political meetings (Thursdays), or the Friday night sisterhood dances.

Week nights, the meetings generally end around midnight, and Sammie and her friends and colleagues go dancing at Sue and Nan's, a private feminist club. Sammie loves to dance. ("It's my release—it's better than sleep.") After a few hours of laughing and joking and talking and dancing and listening to the music (or a quick trip home to the apartment of one of her three steady lovers; that's right, three—no strings on Sammie) Sammie is back *again* on the el train, taking the late-night local, with a final transfer that sometimes takes a while at Ninety-Fifth Street, before she's at last home, for a few hours of sleep before the alarm rings again at 6 A.M.

"It's a treadmill," Sammie admits in a voice that astonishingly betrays no weariness, as she watches Gwenna play with the eyeless doll. She wants to talk about Gwenna. When Gwenna was born, a far more typical childhood seemed to await her—a comfortable home in downstate Illinois, tall elms in the back yard for tree houses and tire swings, a neighborhood with playgrounds and swimming pools, pets and other children.

Sammie worries that Gwenna, this year, can't be in a very good (but very expensive) nearby nursery school; worries that Gwenna's clothing isn't warm enough (her winter jacket is rather threadbare, plucked one Saturday from the free box at the women's center); worries that Gwenna's playthings aren't the most stimulating (whispers that all she can plan to give Gwenna for Christmas is a "rainy-day kit" of paper, glue, sequins, and other odds and ends from around the house—there simply is *no money*); worries that this year the grandparents won't send a Christmas check. They did last year, but that was before they knew the reason why Sammie and her husband got divorced. "They hate me now," says Sammie rather matter-of-factly. Sammie is a lesbian.

Lesbian. At the word, Sammie's eyes sparkle the way Gwenna's might at mention of the word Christmas. Lesbianism was "a surprise package" for Sammie, "as I imagine it was for ninety percent of us who are now women-identified women. It's something we never knew was there, turned our very thoughts away from it, that's how

much we were taught to *fear* the very idea. . . .But the
idea was there, waiting to be discovered, filled with de-
lights and—*riches*. Yes, riches. It sustains, like nourish-
ment; it animates, like electricity. Along with feminism,
lesbianism is my *identity*. I never had a *self* until I knew I
could love women. . . ."

In the days before the American Psychiatric Association decided that homosexuality was "a variation, not an
abnormality," psychiatrists would no doubt have
scrutinized Sammie's childhood in search of dark hints of
maladjustment, incidents that dropped into her personal
life as seeds of abnormality, psychic fingerprints left from
parental errors. . . .

They might have found a few.

Her father, a strong and handsome traveling salesman
whose amorous successes were more notable and numer-
ous than his financial ones, was "a mixture of some characters from *Death of a Salesman* and *Glass Menagerie*—he
fell in love with long distances, all right; one of his trips
turned out to be a final one. Just like in the play, we only
got postcards. Mine said, 'See you someday soon, Sara.'
I've still got it. . . ."

When in high school, vigorous, attractive Sara was
often a lead dancer; her dance coach took a special interest
in her—and seduced her. Out of her teens and into college,
Sara (she was still *Sara* then) had experienced men as not
entirely trustworthy characters; though attracted to men
who physically resembled her father, she drew back from
involved relationships (projected fear of incest provoking
rejection of all males, some psychiatrist might have said)
and placed more trust in women, who, like her mother,
were less likely to exploit and abandon than were dance-
coach father figures. "I was that rare bird in the college

dorm who wouldn't cancel plans with girl friends at the last minute if a guy asked me out for a Coke," Sammie recalls.

Still, she was popular enough, and married in her senior year, continued her studies in comradeship with her husband, pursued an interest in the arts (that remains today in yearning for tickets to operas and concerts and hasty "once a month, about" visits to art galleries along Michigan Avenue where the 157 Sheridan Road bus stops and where "they stare at me because of the way I'm dressed")—and produced a child.

There was a move to a downstate Illinois town: Husband Gene went to work, Sara joined a bridge club and learned to cook. She also had another child, a boy.

Years later the journey from the suburbs to the subways began, in 1968, when a women's consciousness-raising group was organized by a visiting lecturer on the college campus in Sara's town. To Sara was passed the torch by the visiting lecturer (along with the sheaf of New York Radical Feminist "Guidelines for Consciousness Raising.") Sara joked to a friend, "Well, if this is such a good idea, then this town needs *two*," stopped to think about that, and in fact did organize separate groups—one on campus, the other in her own suburban neighborhood, where she cajoled and persuaded everyone on her block to join.

"It started then."

Ordinarily Sammie's talk is as rapid and staccato as machine-gun fire. Now she starts to speak reflectively, more slowly, asks for a cigarette. . . ."Well, we talked about our problems with our husbands, how bored we were with the housework and the playgrounds, how *dominated* we felt, how powerless to escape what we were doing. All of us had talents, none of us were really using them. Oh, one woman had quite a good job as a hospital administrator, but she turned her salary over to her husband, who doled out an allowance to her. And even though they both worked long hours, he came home and relaxed and she came home and cooked and cleaned and changed the beds and put away the laundry and ran their social life. She claimed her job made her independent, but the rest of us had learned to see through that. 'You may be independent from nine to five, Laura,' I told her, 'but at night you just go home and bake gingerbread and wiggle.'

"And, speaking of wiggling, we of course got around to discussing our sex lives. None of us was satisfied. All of us were impatient and frustrated by the artificial, seductive, role-playing 'wiggling' we had to go through. . . .

"Laura . . . let me tell you about Laura. . . .

"There are several incidents that probably are important. . . . One time at our church, after a dinner, we women who were in CR stayed afterward to talk with the minister. We'd found CR so valuable; could the church offer something similar to husbands *and* wives, we wondered?

"The minister was rather jovial; he said he had his own idea of a good consciousness-raising question, and wondered if we'd all be willing to call the husbands back into the room and try to answer it, right then and there.

"The question was, 'If you could be anyone in the world, who would you like to be?' It's probably of political significance that all the men said they were content being who they were, and all the women could think of lots of other people who we'd rather be, if of course we had the choice.

"I said 'The person I'd like to be is Laura.'

"Everybody yelled, acted astounded: 'That's like saying you want to be *yourself*,' one of the women insisted,

'You and Laura are so much alike.' Well, just what was the significant difference, everyone asked. It wasn't her job, her husband, it wasn't any of her talents or skills or strengths or sense of fun—we really *were* very similar in that we had a variety of interesting activities, were well liked. . . .

"Finally, struggling to explain, what I came out with was, *'But she's so beautiful.'*

"Hah. Do you get it? There I was, you see, supposedly consciousness-raised, but suddenly revealed to still be in the 'physical beauty' mental trap! The minister's question had been a damned good one, though I'd thought it was simplistic at first!

"I guess . . . this caused me to begin reflecting on just how aware I was of Laura's beauty. She's very slender. I remembered how outraged I'd been, how sad for her, when she spoke of trying to disguise her slenderness, even wearing padded bras under her negligees in order to try to meet her husband's casual yen for centerfold types. . . Oh, the more I got to know Laura the more I resented her husband, Mel. His own appearance was *gross*, just gross, whereas she was so delicate. Every part of her was delicate. . . .

"I also remembered how aware I was of her incredibly expressive hands. I remembered how she seemed to use them continually, to gesture as she talked: She wouldn't just light a cigarette, she would brandish the match in a large circular movement before bringing it to meet the cigarette tip. . . .

"Maybe anybody else who watched her as closely as I did would have called her manner of gesturing *affected*. To me it was graceful and grand, beautiful and elegant. Most of all . . . I recalled the times I had restrained an impulse to hold or squeeze her hand when we were having a serious talk together. The truth was, I admired Laura greatly, and one reason for my admiration was her beauty.

"In my own mind I used the word 'admiration,' not 'attraction,' and this was a very conscious distinction, because I also consciously thought to myself, 'This is not a sexual attraction, it's partly admiration and maybe even partly envy. It is *not sexual attraction.*

"Then the evening came in our CR group when we discussed lesbianism. The guidelines which gave the evening topic read, 'How do you feel about women loving women, about women whom you know to be lesbians? Have you yourself ever been attracted to another woman? Could you imagine yourself in such a situation? Discuss dreams, fantasies, etc.' "

Sammie's smile, when she is nervous or excited, doesn't move gradually across her face, doesn't grow, it's *there*, all at once, like a light being turned on. Blink. On/off. She smiles like that now, several times in rapid succession. Eyes flashing, she tosses her hair back, pulls herself up to sit cross-legged on the sofa. Smiles, almost laughs, remembering, then suddenly looks serious again.

"Usually, we took our time with the questions. The CR night was, for each of us, *the* most important night of the week. Our testimony was important to us. We were knowing other women, and allowing ourselves to be known to each other as never before. So we explored each topic thoroughly, left nothing even in the far corners of our minds, rummaged everything out.

"But the night we discussed lesbianism was different. One by one, everybody said something like, 'Well, no, I haven't known any women like that personally, not ever, but I think that it's wrong for women like that to be discriminated against, I think women like that should be able to express their preference publicly and be able to live openly. It's not for me, you understand, but for women who are like that I say *right on.*' "

Some scorn or sadness is in Sammie's voice as she recalls this. "Do you realize, do you understand that I'm being extremely accurate? This is total recall, believe me. 'Women like that' indeed. Wow, we zipped through that topic in *fifteen minutes*. Nobody had more than a minute or two of words to say about lesbianism.

"Then it was my turn, and I should have known better, but in I plunged. I said, 'Look, I wonder if we're not forgetting what CR is all about. Can we possibly be being honest with ourselves? Hasn't any one of you who's spoken ever considered lesbianism, ever thought about it? The whole point of this group is to speak not in general terms but to speak *personally*, in terms of our thoughts and feelings, and nobody here has yet tonight, but *I've got to!*'

"Well, the room was quiet as a grave, and nobody looked at me, and I said, 'Look, I haven't got any big bombshells to drop or anything, but I personally just can't say that lesbianism is fine for others but of course it's not for me. We've all talked about sexual dissatisfactions with our husbands and a few of us have looked for answers in affairs with other men, and I simply can't say for sure that I wouldn't consider an affair with another woman.

"Laura looked about to faint. I seem to remember —and this part may not be accurate—I seem to remember every woman in that room reaching for a cigarette, even those who didn't smoke. Then all of them started yelling at me, laughing all at once and saying things like 'Oh, Sammie is kidding us. . . . She's trying to put us on. . . . Why, Sammie, you're the *sexiest* one of all of us. . . . Why,

Sammie, you started sleeping with men at age fourteen. . . .' Then Laura just got up and walked away. Then people started excusing themselves. Even the woman whose house we were in suddenly remembered an errand she had to do.

"An *errand*. On *CR night!* I was so stunned by the speed with which everybody cleared out of there that it didn't even hit me till I was in my car! We usually finished our CR topic about eleven-thirty P.M. and only broke up reluctantly sometime after midnight or as late as one A.M., and then usually only under the pressure of a phone call from somebody's husband; and this time there we all were, *running* for our cars, and it was barely nine o'clock.

"I didn't go back to the group the next week, or the week after that, and nobody called me. But my daydreams about Laura were turning into nightmares by then, because I very quickly figured it out that while I was hurt that nobody called me, I was hurt in a very special way by the fact that *Laura* hadn't called me.

"I was thirty years old then; I had three children. But I felt like a fifteen-year-old kid who was jilted and confused and unpopular. I've no idea what I did during those two weeks away from the group. I'm sure I must have done the usual things—cooked, shopped, played with the kids, took them to play school and lessons and the pediatrician. . . . It's just that I have no recollection of it, none of it. I'm sure I talked to my husband every night, but don't remember a word of that either. Being suddenly separated from the women of my group, I realized that *they* had become my world, more than my husband or home or children.

"There is one thing I remember. Laura. I remember

planning what I would say to her when, *if* I saw her, if I ran into her, if she called, if I heard from her. I planned how I'd laughingly explain how I hadn't meant what I had said at all, and about ten times a day I dialed Laura's number, all but the last digit. I lost eight pounds.

"I was being very tender and cuddly with my husband during this time, I do remember *that*, partly to try to deny what I knew with greater and greater certainty to be the truth—that is, that I was in love with Laura—and partly because I felt somewhat like a severely wounded animal who simply needed creature comfort.

"I tentatively made up my mind to go back to the group on the third Tuesday. I kept changing my mind about what I'd say—I just felt, though, that I couldn't stand it not to be in touch again. But late that Monday night—I couldn't sleep at all—I suddenly woke my husband up and asked him if we couldn't move. 'Where to?' he asked sleepily. 'Where do you want to move to, Sammie?'

" 'Chicago?'

" 'Chicago it is. Now go to sleep.'

"The next morning, he surprised me by remembering that. He looked at me sort of strangely at breakfast and said, 'Do you really want to move?'

" 'Yes.'

" 'Why?'

" 'Because—' (something inside me had the lie ready)'—I think I've gotten too involved with the women's movement here. I feel dragged down. I want a change.' Feeling my way into the lie, I continued, 'That's why I've stopped going to CR. I want for just the two of us to move someplace else, just us and the kids. I just want to be a housewife again.'

" 'We'll move if you want to, Sammie. And we'll move wherever you want to. But I want you to tell me the real reason.'

"*I told him.*

"Believe it or not, *he* was the only one who seemed to understand, who wasn't shocked. He just said, 'Well, don't worry about it, Sammie. Think it over and try to work it out in your own head.' He kissed me. 'We'll work it out to-night.'

" 'But tonight I have CR,' I blurted.

" 'But you just said—*oh!*' We both laughed. 'Okay then, we'll work it out afterward. Have a good day.'

" 'Hey, why are you so cheerful?' I yelled as he was at the door and I was practically in tears of gratitude. 'Just why the hell are you so cheerful? Do you realize that maybe you're married to a lesbian?'

" 'Wait till I tell you about my gambling habit,' he yelled back.

"I loved him.

"Now, I'd love to be able to tell you that my husband's understanding made my passion for Laura disappear—or, rather, I'm sure you'd love to hear that, because it would be very dramatic. It would probably be equally dramatic for me to be able to say that Laura finally realized her passion for *me* and we made it together before Gene and I left town.

"Nothing that cataclysmic. I somehow *knew* I was a lesbian, or a potential lesbian. I also knew I couldn't be honest about this in that town's environment. I went through the CR meeting that night pretending, right along with everybody else, that what had happened the last time I was there hadn't really happened at all. I finally gave that little speech I had so carefully rehearsed. . . .

"Now, Gene, I figured, was willing to move, partly

because he loved me, and partly because he figured if I was going to 'come out' and get to be a big pain in the ass, then he *and* I—and, not incidentally, the kids—would be better off in a bigger community where my 'habit' would be either more easily accepted or more easily hidden. Who knows, maybe he was even thinking he could find a new wife more easily. . . . Gene's very businesslike! But whatever his reasons, I was delighted!

"Actually, we were both starting to nurture quite different fantasies. He figured he was 'man enough' to win out over my changes of thinking, particularly in a new environment where we'd be closer together with fewer outside friends—and *I* started to imagine that after we moved, Laura would come to visit me (which she would have to do, we'd been such close friends), that she'd somehow leave all her inhibitions behind her in Bloomington and we'd have a glorious sometime affair in Chicago. . . .

"The only reality to come out of all these vagaries is that we did, in fact, move. To Chicago. I linked up immediately with every feminist group I could find: a women's gynecological self-help clinic, an abortion referral service, the NOW committee that was working on ratification of the ERA—and *of course* I joined a new CR group.

"The fact that I was attracted to other women became ever clearer to me. And it stopped being funny to Gene. No, that's the wrong word. It was never funny to him, but he'd been able at first to treat it with good-natured sympathy. That stopped the night my new CR group met at our house. Whereas my group in Bloomington had been all straight—heterosexual, that is—my Chicago group was about half lesbian, some of them being what Gene could only see as frightening stereotypes.

"He gently introduced the idea of his moving out,

though I wasn't too anxious for it, and in fact was somewhat afraid of it. Still, perhaps he understood the nature of my own growth as well or better than I did; perhaps he even helped me face it. The truth was, I did not define myself as "his wife" anymore. The truth also was that sex was important to me, and as I looked back I saw that all the sexual relationships I'd ever had with men had been nonorgasmic. I wasn't bitter about it or anything; I simply wanted to explore what seemed to be my true sexual nature.

"Also, though I tried not to take it out on Gene, I was developing a good deal of hostility toward men, a *political* hostility, not an irrational anger. It's true enough that the liberation of women will mean the liberation of men from their constraining role as Oppressor, but let's not kid ourselves that most men will welcome this liberation, since it will mean giving up the power all of them have been taught to want and the exercise of which many of them enjoy!

"Now, it has been explained to me very earnestly that male *and* female roles are learned: Thus the male is not the enemy by virtue of his male biology, but because he rationalizes his supremacy on the basis of biological difference, making the *role* the enemy, not the man. I don't buy this reasoning, because men don't have to buy that rationalization! I *am* a radical, I *am* a separatist.

"My thinking is *very separatist*. Some feminists look forward to all-female environments, communities of women. I'm one of these. We are stronger because we're women and because we're lesbians; we have had to be stronger to cope with this society. I've chosen to live with women, work with women. I love my sisters; I love being a lesbian; I love working and fighting for lesbian feminist rights. I want to share only with women, be only with women. I don't want men around me—I don't want to be hassled by them. They're fine in their own universe, I don't want them in mine. I don't *hate* men, I simply don't *like* them. . . .

"Gene saw this coming sufficiently so that he didn't even try to introduce me to his new business community, never once asked me to entertain or go to a business dinner once we got here. His only form of oppression is subtle, even now; to anybody outside the movement it would look very good indeed.

"He comes to see me, comes to see the kids. He notices I haven't had my hair cut and my hair used to look gorgeous, used to mean a lot to me when I had it cut well. He notices that I'm wearing tacky clothing, when I used to love silk shirts (I had them in half a dozen colors, but they've all worn out now).

"How does he react to this? He reacts by saying, 'Let me give you some money to have your hair done, let me buy you some shirts.'

"That's a potentially exploitative gesture, a potentially exploitative act. It can't be excused even if he means it kindly: Its effect is both to reinforce his role as benefactor and mine as recipient, and he's choosing what he offers so as to give me, again, some aspects of traditional "feminine" gorgeousness.

"Is the *act* the enemy? Or is *he*? He is, because he's making the offer. Of course I reject it."

Sammie's hair, now, is shoulder-length and un-kempt. Sammie, now, wears only sweatshirts, sometimes two at a time: Chicago in the winter can be cruelly cold. . . .

"How does it look to you?" she wonders cheerfully. "All this squalor?"

The answer is both obvious and impossible. The bare floor is grimy, one chair leg broken, the children's cardboard play table lopsided and torn. The sofa is coming apart not just at seams but in the middle of the cushions; a Hoover portable dryer is disconnected, needs to be repaired, and probably won't be. *That's* how it looks to me, or at least that's a fair physical description. Whether or not the room is squalid is irrelevant, in functional terms: squalor is what drags one down, pulls whole segments of the personality under—and that's not happening here. Sammie could be evicted, could run out of food stamps, see these sticks of weak-limbed furniture collapse—and just keep going. . . .

"And how does it *sound* to you?" Sammie asks me directly, challenging. "How does it sound to you if I telescope together all my militancy? 'Come the revolution, we'll get rid of the men,' " she quotes herself. " 'Every time I look at my son I wish he were a daughter instead'? *Hopeless*, right?" she guesses cheerfully, without the slightest hint of the paranoia with which some minority women would ask that question—minority women who've learned too painfully the truth of Joan Didion's baldly stated admission, "A writer is always selling somebody out." Women like Sammie can't be sold out.

No, I don't think you're hopeless, Sammie. Strange, not hopeless. In your own terms I'd have to count you one of the successes. I believe you when you say you're completely free of dependencies and depressions: that you "fit inside your skin now," whereas before there was a constant sense of masquerade, constant efforts to smooth off all the rough edges and fit inside a niche that eventually seemed like a prison cell. You've found *yourself*, and no matter how strange your life looks to me, it works for you, and I imagine it will continue to. Just as soon as you've pulled your children through their childhoods, you'll head straight for your own vision of the future, and make that work too: at

seventy, you'll be a peppery old lady in a separatist com-
mune with other peppery old ladies, working away at your
revolution. You'll survive.

But what about the children? Sammie is calling
Gwenna now, looking around for Gwenna's boots and
parka—it's almost time to leave. Look around the room
now, for Gwenna's doll and truck and sandwich bag; dust
off the toys, the floor was dirty; *run* or we'll miss the 11:08
111A bus, *run*. Gwenna, eager for lunchtime, takes a bite
of her sandwich as we run, holding it with half the sandwich
bag, unknowingly creating potential for a small disaster
—for just as we board the bus it lurches, Gwenna loses her
balance, and the sandwich falls on the floor! Quickly, with
an offhand gesture that sums up her ability to cope with
setbacks, large or small, Sammie just picks up the sandwich, tosses away the part that touched the floor, folds the
remaining sticky piece of bread in two, seals the bag this
time, tells Gwenna "You've got a new sandwich
now. . . . But it's only half, because it fell. . . . But you'll
be more careful not to fall next time, because you balance
yourself, see, like this. . . ."

Gwenna nods intently, focusing on her mother's face.

Gwenna will learn to be a survivor, too; at least she's
learning a lot about survival, even now. She clutches the
sandwich bag firmly now; the bus jerks away from the Londale stop. And this time Gwenna does not fall.

Rona:

"Women Leave You Too"

Even to those of us who'd grown accustomed to the battle-fatigue dress of some New York radical women, Rona's appearance came as a shock: Heads jerked back, as from a well-placed blow. Rona's dungarees were discolored, torn at both knees so that one lower pants-leg was almost detached; layers of thin sweaters sent frayed long sleeves of different colors down to her arms, yet none quite reached the wrists. She wore no coat, although the November evening was bitterly cold. A towel was wrapped around her neck in place of a muffler; she untied and removed this as she entered the top-floor Charles Street walk-up, and folded it carefully as she sat down, smoothing it after it was folded.

This was the first meeting of a new consciousness-raising group, and as always at such meetings a yearning to share one's feelings seemed punctuated with impulses of nervous suspicion. The suspicion is always heighted as the facilitator gently explains that it is to be expected some women present this first night will drop out over succeeding weeks, leaving only a core group. Everyone glances around the circle, questions in the eyes: Who will the dropouts be? Will they drop out because they find us—*me*—pathetic, beyond rescue—sick? Will even those who remain disapprove, render silent scornful judgment, of *fail to keep confidence*? That's the real fear to anyone about to reveal herself to a group of women who, for now, are strangers: *Will someone tell*?

Such inchoate feelings of nervousness lost focus when Rona entered, replaced by new fears, still undefined, but centered just on Rona. Her appearance was no doubt the cause. Simply, her attire conformed to no norm at all, made no conscious social statement. It was neither revolutionary, counterrevolutionary, nor traditional. Did it reflect extreme poverty, the unconcern of the artist, or madness? Or all of these? Like Van Gogh's hostesses, we worried about some irrational act that this poor young woman might be capable of; even in this avant-garde circle, we realized we carried some middle-class sense of propriety.

We all kept glancing at her as we gave our own "who I am and why I'm here" testimony, and Susan (the facilitator for the evening) kept filling her coffee cup apprehensively. Rona didn't seem totally in control, at times seemed to close her eyes and doze off, yet her posture didn't seem that of someone about to fall asleep. Rather, she seemed trancelike.

Finally it was her turn to speak. She seemed to engage in a palpable struggle to get her voice and thoughts wrenched free. "My name is Rona and I'm a poet. . . . and I'm here to talk about *pain.*" She contracted her upper body as she almost screamed the last word, then was quiet a minute, collecting herself to continue. "Now, let me try to get this to you clear. See, certain things—conditions —were handed to me: handed to me as a woman alone, as a working woman, as an urban woman, *as a woman, period.* These things . . . came with the territory, more or less; and when they were given to me they weren't given one at a time but all strung together, but loosely, with a lot of gaps, like an old and ugly strand of pearls.

"Here is what these things—conditions—were. They were: Discrimination. Failure. Rejection. And always being exploited somehow, always, by men. *And then there were the gaps where there was nothing–nothing.* Does anybody else know what that's like? Is anybody here with me?" A few heads nodded, tentatively. Others of us plainly didn't identify or understand.

"Okay then. What I needed was something to fill in the gaps, the gaps between those rotten pearls. If they were to be the conditions of my life, then at least something had to make them hold together. *Something* had to be found to help me live, to get me through, to get me through from one bad deal to the next, from one night to the next morning. And maybe the *something* I was looking for—whatever it was—would not only hold the strand of my life together, but eventually make the flawed ornaments of my existence dissolve and disappear, or change their nature somehow.

"This substance—this thing that I was looking for—I thought it was called love. Now I know its name is *pain.*

"I thought a man would be the answer. A man—to love me and either shield me from the defeats or share them with me. I never found a man who'd even talk to me about my work or poems, though, who cared at all about the doors that were closed to me. Oh, get it straight that they *pretended* to. . . . Men! Believe me, I've been through it all with men. . . ."

She gulped her cooled coffee greedily before continuing, asked with a gesture for a cigarette. Calmer, she continued.

"In literature, remember, there used to be this thing called *courtship*? Quaint, huh? No, it's really there, it's just that it's women now who have to do the courting. I used to waste my whole life's energy, day in, day out, when I wasn't doing temporary office work to help myself get by, to pay the rent, to scrape together enough cash to buy myself two weeks free of the nine-to-five, so I could write. Except until the poetry was successful, I needed, somehow, a *man*.

"I tried, I courted. Plan, compromise. You'll come to dinner? Okay, I'll shop for dinner. You can't come tonight? Okay, then what about tomorrow?

"Wait, live in limbo, don't go out in case the phone rings. . . .say things you don't mean, spend money you can't afford, have your hair done, try the bars.

"You do it right: he says 'Do I know you from somewhere?' and you say 'Ah, I don't think you know me *yet*,' and something seems to start. Hell, did I really think somebody would learn to love me over a glass of beer at Maxwell's Plum? She stroked the folded towel.

"Well then, maybe somebody could learn to love me at a different kind of bar. . . . I started to read the movement literature, read *The Ladder*, and *Rat* and *Off Our Backs*, felt maybe it was impossible for a woman with any sensitivity—and I am a sensitive woman—to relate to a man the way things are today; maybe I was more attuned, potentially, to love another woman. 'Lesbianism is the logical extension of feminism,' *right*? 'Feminism is the theory, lesbianism is the practice,' *right*?

"Things—little things—had begun to happen to make the possibility of love with another woman seem natural to me. For one thing, I had close friendships with some women, just a few, and some incidents that seemed. . . .like talismans.

"Once at Maxwell's Plum I was sitting near this girl, and we were approached by two guys—real pigs!—I think from Dayton; and we strung them along for a while, then started laughing and making faces at each other because their attitude was so ludicrous, so smug, so blatant. She said to me, 'Look, why don't the two of us go someplace else?' We walked to a little restaurant called *Grass* and had soup and coffee and just talked. It was really *genuine*. 'Well, here we've been, two huntresses putting away their weapons for the night and giving up the chase,' I said as we left the restaurant. 'Well, at least we haven't gone *hungry*,' she said. We shook hands and left. But I had a fleeting thought that maybe I should have asked her where she lived, that it might have been comforting to ask her to spend the night. It only occurred to me later that "hungry" the way she said it might have been a sexual pun. But it maybe wasn't. Her name was Anne. That's all I know about her.

"And then at work there was a girl that I began to fantasize about.

"And then once at a speak-out, for some reason I went dressed up, in a suit and high heels, and some woman in jeans said 'Hi, gorgeous,' and I reacted on some instinctive level, got a sexual thrill just like I would have if a man had said it.

"But it was at a dance I went to—only women—when I danced close to another woman, I felt good. I knew then there's a lot of potential feeling for one another women *can* have, but never get a chance to know about. Opportunities like women's dances are too rare. . . . Finally I had read or heard something that made sense to me—about how the plan is to allow the forbidden, to learn to love the *woman in ourselves*, by loving other women.

"I was really ready for an affair when Rachel came to work at my office. She was divorced, no nonsense to her. She came on to me—flirted, teased me. I responded.

"I did something, after about a week—ah, I still can't believe I did it! Cheap trick. I got coy, asked her to change my typewriter ribbon for me, just to see if she would. She did. Her fingers got covered with ink. . . .I handed her a tissue, felt childish and romantic and ashamed.

"Would she come to my apartment for dinner? Yes . . . and the difference between inviting her and inviting a guy was that I *knew she'd come!* There was a trust between us right away, that I'd never felt before with men. She began to come for dinner almost every night; I shopped like crazy. Ah, Italian food, Cuban food, paella, and we'd always have a bottle of wine with dinner and talk afterward, later and later. Eventually she brought some clothing so she could stay over; eventually she moved in.

"But get it straight that we didn't sleep together right away: get that straight—it's important. Nothing like that could ever happen with a *man*, you see. We touched each other, we'd stand naked together in front of the mirror sometimes; we'd brush each other's hair, we'd bathe each other, help each other dress and undress, more at first like sisters than lovers. But there was the certainty that we didn't need to speak out loud—the certainty that we did love each other; but it was a love that didn't carry any sense of urgency. There wasn't that frightening, sometimes ugly sense of haste there was with *men*. . . ." (There was some distaste in the way she'd say the words "man" or "men." Not unique—Margaret Sloan in a major address admitted "It hurts me to say the word 'husband.' " Not unique at all. So common in fact that one comes close to accepting the master-slave analogy the women's movement is so fond of. It's perhaps no mere rhetorical trick: Many women feel sufficiently victimized by men that their tone of voice when

referring to the male sex seems identical to the way Rap
Brown said "whitey.")

"We took our time, we got to know each other, so very
slowly. We were like sleepwalkers and our time together
like a dream. She was so lovely. It was so different. I'd
never exactly lived with a man before, but men had stayed
with me for days at a time, like stray pets, with me feeding
and serving them. With Rachel—well, neither one of us
had been brought up to exploit, to demand or expect service. We served each other in little ways, did kindnesses
for each other, got each other little gifts. . . . Do you understand what it can be like to do that, with no worry about
stepping out of bounds, making the first gesture when *you*
felt like it but resisting because *he* should? We bought each
other surprises, little love gifts. We shopped together,
bought   new   sheets   and   pillowcases,   always
preparing. . . . She'd had affairs with women before but
said that this was different, that this had even more tenderness than her best relationships. I was jealous, hearing her
talk of other lovers—but proud, too, since she was with me
now.

"And when we did sleep together as lovers it was so
warm and gentle. And since I hadn't slept with a woman
before, I sat up and asked her afterward if I had done things
right. . . . And she laughed softly and held me, and then
we both laughed. And that was my answer, assuming I had
even meant the question. . . .

"Ah, I'd never been so happy. Sex had always seemed
cheap to me with men, since it was never linked to friendship. There was never any tenderness or laughter. Rachel
and I, because we lived *and* worked together, had everything, including, of course, our lovely secret. And we *did*

keep it secret, of course, at the office. We quietly enjoyed the effect that each of us had on men. Even sometimes when a man would ask one of us out, we'd make him take us both out, and he'd think "Super!"—oh you could tell how he was hoping the evening would end. But then afterward we'd both pretend modesty and tell him good night, then get into *separate cabs*, and meet back at the apartment, laughing.

"We got to know the gay community a little, though. And while it didn't bother me to see Rachel flirt with a guy at work, I'd die a little if, at a dance, another woman danced with her. . . . But during those months we were together, I worked so well, so well.

"And wrote so many poems. One night, though, she told me she had to meet a friend after work, a friend from out of town, from Buffalo, her home town. And she didn't come home that night, and apologized the next day, of course—but apologized *without explaining*.

"I needed an explanation. And that was when the pain I'd always felt came back, the first pain in so long: because I wanted to demand an explanation, but I didn't dare.

"I realized then that I felt 'married' to her, asked her if when my lease came up for renewal, she'd sign it with me. She said she'd think about it, but always avoided the subject whenever I brought it up, and started to seem strange and distant. One night—no, well, one afternoon at work —she told me she was going home early to shop and get dinner ready. That was nothing unusual, since it was her week to fix the dinners. But when I got home—when I got home, her things were gone.

"Ah, it all went bad from there. I couldn't stay at that job any more, couldn't write without her, tried to talk things out, tried to look for the same tenderness I'd known with her, with other women. But you know, the Duchess can be just as depressing as Maxwell's Plum. . . . I ought to interject here that I used to be pretty, see, used to take a lot of time with my appearance. And when a woman did pay attention to me at a bar or dance, I started to catch on that I was just—sometimes, to her—a sex object. That's the only way I can think of to put it.

"How often I'd complained about men who never took any time to get to know me, never cared what I had to say. It was so surprising to find the same thing could be true with women. If you don't want to be kissed, a woman who forces a kiss can be just as much of a pig as a man; all in all, *that* is the worst thing I found out.

"Out of a lot of bad things, the very worst that happened was that I got drunk one night, just from being sad, and woke up the next morning in this house in Riverdale, with a little child saying, '*Mommy, Mommy!*' and trying to wake up the woman who was asleep with one arm and one leg thrown across me. I didn't even know who that woman was. . . .

"I decided that I'd have no more affairs with anybody, men or women. It was a sudden decision. I think I made it as I was going out the revolving door of this Riverdale apartment building: I went through that revolving door and came out in another country. Something snapped. All the old searches, I knew, were over. There wasn't any magic, in the end, about trying to love women. Women can be tender and gentle, yes, like Rachel was. But women can fuck you over just as much. Women leave you too. . . .

"That was about two years ago. After I became . . . celibate . . . I felt a little freer and better. I was out of a trap, free of searching and pretending. I can only compare it, I guess, to escaping this culture's high view of classical music. I never liked it, I was never interested in it. Let other people talk about the beauty and the tone and rhythm and say that it's beautiful and cultural and produces expansion of the spirit, and that the emotional response to it is uplifting. . . . For me, those feelings just aren't there. Can anybody understand that? And it's the same with sex. As far as concerts are concerned, I don't want to go to them. As far as sex is concerned, I don't want to do it.

"I think I've conditioned myself completely out of wanting sex; I used to have sexual dreams a lot—even that doesn't happen any more. Sometimes I yearn for just nonsexual tenderness and touching. I guess I'd like to find that. I guess I'd like to find somebody who just wanted that, who could understand me, and take care of me a little. Because sometimes I'm still so very lonely. . . ."

The Lesbian Connection

Interviewer: You seem to paint a rosy picture.
Lesbian: Life is not rosy. Lesbianism is.[1]

Feel the real glow that comes from "our" sisterhood.
We can teach you something about being gentle and
kind for we have never felt competitive. Remember we
long before you have known discontent with male
society and we long before you knew and appreciated
the full potential of everything female. . . . It is we
who say welcome to you, long blind and oppressed
sisters, we have been fighting against male supremacy
for a long time. Join us.[2]

The above claims do not represent isolated attitudes, but most pervasive ones, which seem to radiate
insistently, like heartthrobs, through the body of the
feminist movement: in literature, certainly—in the news-
letters, anthologies, and pamphlets. Yet the call to lesbianism exists more as a felt presence than as the printed
word—at every gathering, sometimes in a restrained form,
sometimes in a more aggressive mode, but always *there*.
Typical scenarios: The 1974 NOW Sexuality Conference
where lesbians took the microphone to complain that only
20 percent of the workshops were oriented toward gay
women; the 1975 Media Women's Conference where a lesbian of delicate features in stark black suit accented with
lavender arm band came forward to protest that no
member of the panel was a lesbian, demanded the right to
sit on stage, since "even though I have no remarks prepared I must sit with this group as a physical reminder that
my sisters and I have been invisible for too long."

The contemporary women's movement was not organized around lesbian rights, probably for no more esoteric reason than the fact that Betty Friedan and other founders of NOW—the modern counterpart of National American Women Suffrage Association—are not lesbians. In fact, in an effort to contend that women's liberation was totally compatible with traditional "womanliness," Friedan and other conservatives in the late sixties and early seventies took pains to stress that lesbianism was *not* a cause, concern, or focus. (Conservative efforts to submerge any lesbian identity for the cause ranged from admitting that it might be an incidental or related issue to dismissing the thought with epithets such as "Lavender Menace.") In denying any lesbian orientation, however, early movement women brought about the very effect they had hoped to avoid: They *mobilized* gay women to insist on a role in the movement by giving lesbians cause to contend that the women's movement itself oppressed and ignored them.

Women's liberation mobilized lesbian liberation in another way as well—by simply setting up "respectable" ways and means of challenging male dominance in social and economic arenas. Eventually the mainstream feminist movement, represented by NOW, and the underground lesbian movement which had since the late 1960s been forming its own ad hoc organizations such as D.O.B. (Daughters of Bilitis, a group which predates the feminist movement and which offers personal help and guidance to gay women), had to either conflict or converge. After a good many conflicts, well-attended by the press and therefore mutually damaging in terms of public image, both groups tended to shift toward an uneasy liaison.

The reason for the imperfection of this union is obvious: Feminism and lesbianism are simply not the same thing. Feminism is an attempt at either reform or revolution; lesbianism is a sexual and emotional preference. Although women's liberation and lesbian liberation are working toward some common goals, the latter is essentially less political than the former, a simple life-style commitment that *may or may not*, for any individual lesbian, have organic links with the larger struggle for women's legal, economic, and social rights. The insistence by some lesbians that the two minority manifestations *are* synonymous (and further that the lesbian represents feminism's vanguard) can become annoying to straight movement women both for its stridency and its lack of logic.

> *"Lesbians are women who survive without men financially and emotionally," boast some leaders of the lesbian movement, thus representing the ultimate in an independent life style. . . .*
>
> *Lesbians are the women who battle day by day to show that women are valid human beings, not just appendages of men.*
>
> *Lesbians are the women who are penalized for their sexuality more than any other women on earth. . . . to declare oneself a lesbian is still tantamount to a Jew declaring himself in Nazi Germany. . . .*
>
> *Thus it is no wonder that lesbians are attracted to the women's movement, are active in it, and feel they are the vanguard of it.*
>
> *If women's liberation does mean liberation from the dominance of men, lesbians' opinions should be actively sought out, for in many ways the lesbian has freed herself from male dominations.*[3]

Sidney Abbott and Barbara Love make the preceding statements in their essay, "Is Women's Liberation A Lesbian Plot?" One is definitely left with the notion the authors would like to answer their rhetorical question with a firm *Yes*. Their transparently defensive attitude deserves understanding if not excuse: It is a not atypical attitude of lesbians who feel themselves not only discriminated against by a sexist society in general but painfully ignored or at times humiliated by the feminist organizers and organizations. But defensiveness is never an aid to logic, and on examination many of Abbott/Love's confident assertions quickly crumble.

Not only do such insistences annoy straight movement women, they potentially threaten the image of service-oriented moderate gay women's organizations (such as D.O.B.), preempt media attention and thus pry movement emphasis away from more reasoned lesbian writers and researchers; and in final effect thus only *further prejudice* the community at large against lesbianism. Such contentions as Abbott and Love put forth simply need straightening out.

"Lesbians . . . survive without men financially and emotionally, thus representing the ultimate in an independent life style" is something of an overgeneralization. For example, Sammie's emotional independence from men is beyond doubt or question; but no woman is an island economically, and even Sammie is surrounded by a sexist support system. She accepts rent money from her ex-husband, food stamps from a sexist/capitalist economy, and her organization makes use of rent-free office space in a building owned by a man. She in effect lives a highly rarified existence, identifying relevant issues and working to raise public consciousness to some level of awareness of those issues, but she would not be able to function as a crusader were it not for a broad-based economic structure that enables her to meet her basic needs with minimal effort—or at least with no steady, traditional employment.

Second, "Lesbians are the women who battle day by day to show that women are human beings. . . ." No statistics are available, but everyone's direct or indirect experience can confirm that many lesbians don't battle at all: They prefer in fact to conceal their sexual preference and achieve their career goals within standard professional hierarchies while making as few waves as possible. For example, a wealthy, forty-year-old lesbian who is a writer and lives part-time in Europe and part-time in the States spoke of "passing" in an interview with Delores Klaich, and expressed reservations about the gay-rights movement:

> I pass. I pass beautifully. And if you pass, society —people—let you be. After you reach a certain age relatives stop asking when you're going to get married. You've established your identity as a career woman. (Hideous description, I know—*career* woman. Always reminds me of Joan Crawford in a severe suit. . . .) I don't cross-dress. I don't march in parades. That's another part of me. I'm not a joiner, never have been. I'd feel as out of place in a gay-liberation parade as I would, say—oh, say, getting a pedicure.[4]

The following Klaich interview is also typical.

> Klaich: Are you involved in the gay movement?
> Interviewee: No.
> Klaich: How do you feel about this movement?
> Interviewee: Well . . . the same way I feel about not having been active in the peace movement. I feel guilty.
> Klaich: Are you concerned about what straight men and women think of lesbians?
> Interviewee: Personally, I really don't give a damn.[5]

Such interviews from Klaich, who was concerned with portraying the lesbian role as it is *lived* by women rather than as *defined* by "movement women," seem to offer a truer picture than is hastily sketched by Abbott and Love; and the emerging model is clearly one of lesbianism exercised as accommodation within the system, rather than ardent activist efforts to change the system. (Women such as Sammie, who *are* fighters and activists, represent a small minority within a minority; in fact, those who resemble Sammie are extremely few in number.)

Typical too, are stories such as that of Esther, a successful career woman who lives in California and who runs her own contracting firm, very much a "masculine" business. She works with men constantly—

> employs them, plans and deals with them at every level of the construction industry. She is very conscious of being a woman in a man's domain. She is sharp and shrewd, can match wits with the best of them. But she must be careful to maintain her "feminine" image, since the success of her enterprise depends on her being able to command the respect of men in the business. She has an expensive home in the Berkeley Hills where she lives "alone," according to her success story, which was written up in the women's page of the *Oakland Tribune*. Her lover is *totally invisible* to the outside world.[6]

Del Martin and Phyllis Lyon in their book *Lesbian/Woman* offer this and other such stories of lesbian "accommodation."

The impression here is not one of a "battler"; Esther is a professional woman who is not trying to show anyone anything, at least not by political action. And women who lack the relative independence of being recognized writers are even less apt to be doing battle: The fear of discovery that must haunt lesbian workers in routine jobs (say, government civil-service jobs) is a matter of concern for all of us, but not exactly a stimulus to action for most of those in a position to be harmed by the revelation of their life styles.

A young woman such as Rona, for example, while she worked at an office job not only failed to be forthright about her affair with her co-worker, but went to the additional role-playing effort of dating men on occasion in order to create the illusion of standard sexual orientation. Quite a lengthy analysis could probably be written comparing the degree of compromise Rona exhibited with that of her heterosexual sisters, who also role-play, date, and conform to traditional image. The only immediate and obvious difference is that Rona never sleeps with the men she dates. Does this make her a feminist? Or would a feminist insist that all role-playing is sick and submissive; that Rona is no more liberated than the typical hopelessly heterosexual young working woman—they simply sleep in different beds.

Any lesbian like Rona, whose behavior makes it clear that she really has no quarrel with men, but simply does not want to socialize or sleep with them, is also making her personal acceptance of the present system clear. The existence of thousands of these women make such statements as "Feminism is the theory, lesbianism is the practice" seem naive and empty rhetoric, an equation that simply doesn't work. A woman like Rona can no more be thought to be a feminist than Diahann Carroll can be said to be a civil-rights activist. Belonging to an oppressed minority group does not automatically make one a crusader against oppression.

Lesbians are "penalized for their sexuality more than any other women on earth"? Have Ms.'s Abbott and Love checked out the customary treatment of Hindu widows or unfaithful Mohammedan wives? "To declare oneself a lesbian is tantamount to declaring oneself a Jew in Nazi Germany"? *If* lesbians are being systematically deprived of life and property, we certainly ought to know about it—but the fact that Abbott and Love offer not the merest whisper of supporting evidence makes it clear that they do not even take their own charges seriously. They are merely out to agitate through rhetoric. What other point is there to constructing a stereotype of lesbians as militant activists and sexual martyrs?

Finally, "If women's liberation means liberation from the dominance of men, lesbians' opinions should be actively sought out" makes little sense to a woman whose orientation remains heterosexual. By analogy, would black leaders who seek integration gain insights toward their goal by consulting separatists? Should the black and white parents and teachers seeking to integrate Roxbury schools "actively seek out" opinions from either Eldridge Cleaver or the Ku Klux Klan?

The statements from Abbott and Love which have been quoted, however, do make a point, implicitly, by their very exaggeration. In reaction to extreme discrimination, some lesbian writers and movement leaders seem to have developed a group concept of self as superior beings, in style of living if not in essential nature. This is most clearly shown by the claims made by these two women as to the superiority of affection and devotion between two lesbian women:

> Feminists who have men in their lives and are free to demonstrate and fight for equality complain that the wonderful feelings of independence, self-possession, and self-determination they have around other women are shot down when they come home and are dominated by

men in bed. No matter what the feminist does, the physical act throws woman and man back into role-playing;
the male as conqueror asserts his masculinity and the
female is expected to be a passive receiver. All of her
politics are instantly shattered. . . .

By contrast,

Love between equals provides the most fulfilling relationship. An equal experience is an enrichment shared
by two lovers . . . two women who instinctively know
each other's needs and honor them.[8]

The use of the word "instinctively" is a curious departure from feminist vocabulary; also, why do they mention
two women as their only example of "love between
equals"? In fact, is it not rather self-serving social astig-
matism to refuse to acknowledge that lesbian relationships
sometimes fall far short of the ideal?

Can it really be denied that women play power games
too? That women can become possessive, jealous, callous,
and uncaring? That women can seek relationships with
other women for the same compensatory reasons (fear, lack
of ego strength) that propel heterosexual women into premature or unwise marriages or liaisons?

Indeed, some of the comments at a Gay Women's Al-
ternative (GWA) seminar on lesbian marriages in the fall of
1974 might well have been heard at a discussion of traditional, heterosexual marriage:

I need to be protected from feeling alienated and
isolated. . . . I need a one-to-one relationship to feel
secure. . . . I need the reassurance of knowing that
another woman cares enough to commit herself to
me. . . . I need to live with *someone*, and I admit I'm not
always careful enough *who*. . . .

Gay women, like straight women, are perfectly capable of making choices of partners on the basis of a limited criterion, often sex. "The reason I began to sleep with women in the first place," reported a woman named Gina at another GWA meeting, "is that sex is important to me—I'm certainly after intense sexual experiences, and I act often on the basis of sexual attraction and that alone. I'm attracted to some women of a certain physical type; I'm less attracted to women of other types. There's just nothing I can do about this. I've only been gay for a few years and this may change after a time, but for now I have to admit I'm less interested in a woman's soul or personality than in her body."

Perhaps Gina is right in anticipating that her purely physical orientation may change after a time. But perhaps it *won't*. Rona complained of being regarded as a sex object by lesbians, and presumably not all of the women who viewed her as such were newly come-out. Even Jill Johnston is said to have remarked about one woman, "I like her breasts and don't understand her legs."

Gay women, just as straight women, can be guilty of "cheating" on a faithful partner, straying without mutual agreement or permission or any scrupulous rules of open marriage ("I need a lot of deep breaths, a lot of different beds; strict monogamy is stifling," said Gina); of needing to think up hasty excuses on their way home in a cab after midnight; or of exploiting other women in an effort to make up for an instance of rejection. ("I led on every woman I met, for months, trying to get over the fact that the first woman I fell in love with, after I came out, simply didn't fall in love with *me*," a woman explained at another GWA rap meeting.

Lesbians who are also movement women can use feminism as an excuse for, or a technique of, coercion and seduction: not merely by *implying* that lesbianism is the vanguard of feminism, but by *insisting* that any woman who is not a lesbian fails in some crucial way to meet a test of true feminist feeling. Sue Cummings, director of rap sessions at a Manhattan women's health clinic, reports, "In many of our workshops we see that young women these days feel a sense of guilt if they haven't had a lesbian experience." Barbara Harrison concluded in a spring 1974 article in *New York* magazine that lesbianism was a new sex style imperative for women who wanted to be considered serious feminists (it wasn't imperative that lesbianism become your primary sex style, explained Harrison—but one was supposed to at least have given it a serious try). One radical woman noted, "In some circles you're *out* if you're not a lesbian. At a recent conference your commitment was *measured* by whether or not you were a lesbian."[9]

So powerful can this attitude become that it has in many areas created a phenomenon known as *political lesbianism*: A political lesbian has in effect convinced herself that it *is* "right" or "correct" to be a lesbian, that "Gay is good," so she will proclaim herself to be homosexual. But her lesbianism is based on political expediency, not physical impulse. The political lesbian will rarely or never sleep with her sisters: She is celibate. (Challenged by a heterosexual to explain why this is not sheer hypocrisy, she can at least reply that it is no more hypocritical than the behavior of the woman who calls herself heterosexual but in fact rarely takes a partner.)

Challenged by her homosexual sisters to translate her politics into action, she must search for more sophisticated responses and counterstrategy. What can a political lesbian say to such comments as "You oppress me if you refuse to sleep with women" (or even "You oppress me if you refuse to sleep with *me*")? One woman said resignedly, "It's just like it used to be with men—sometimes all you can say is *No*."

Employing political terminology in such a context, translating the language of liberation into the arm-twisting slang of sexual aggression, cheapens both politics and sexual encounter. An Army officer who insisted to women, "Sleep with me to prove your patriotism," would at once be seen to be indulging in tawdry bribery. What of a lesbian who insists, "You ought to sleep with me to prove your feminism"? Is it really so very different?

It takes no very great stretch of deductive powers to imagine that woman/woman relationships, as well as man/woman ones, can be characterized by jealousy, possessiveness, or neurotic need to control. In her analysis of lesbian history, for instance, Klaich writes,

> Among the new facts tumbling out about [Gertrude] Stein's personal life, one of the most astonishing concerns her famous break with Ernest Hemingway. Until recently hardly anyone knew why these two close friends had argued; most assumed it had had something to do with literature. . . . Not so. Hemingway himself wrote "I always wanted to fuck her and she knew it." It is probable that Stein was not entirely unwilling. But Toklas put her foot down. "You know," Toklas told good friend Donald Sutherland shortly before her death, "I made Gertrude get rid of Hemingway." . . . Toklas also told Sutherland that she made Gertrude Stein get rid of another friend, Mabel Dodge.[10]

Toklas's domination of Stein is also implied in a passage of *A Moveable Feast*, when Hemingway tells of overhearing Stein reduced to begging Toklas in these terms: "Don't . . . Don't. Don't. Please don't. I'll do anything, pussy, but please don't do it. Please don't. Please don't, pussy."[11] As Klaich herself surmises, "Toklas was one strong dyke." *This* is "the most fulfilling relationship . . . two women who instinctively know each other's needs and honor them"?

In a somewhat more temperate variation on the theme of troubled lesbian relationships, Vita Sackville-West wrote of the jealously and insecurity that was shown by her lover, Violet. In her diary, she recalled:

> Violet was at Bordighera. . . . In March I went out to join her at Avignon. . . . I hadn't seen her for six weeks. It ought to have been a good meeting but it wasn't. Three hours after my arrival we were already quarreling because she apparently thought she could persuade me to stay with her for good, and was angry when she found she couldn't. We motored from Avignon to Bordighera, and quarreled the whole time, and I was acutely wretched. . . . Then at San Remo I lost my head and said I would stay, and for a few days we were happy. We went on to Venice, but I don't really look back on that journey with much pleasure. She was ill, with a touch of jaundice, a most unromantic complaint, and I could do nothing with her, especially after I had gone back on what I had said at San Remo. . . . I admit that I behaved badly over that. One ought not to allow oneself the luxury of losing one's head. . . .[12]

Such incidents illustrate some of the least generous attitudes of any love relationship: possessive domination; shallowness of surface attraction, by which standards jaundice is "an unromantic illness"; the calculated advice to "not lose one's head"; the unfortunate exercise of neurotic need and false promise.

Really ordinary stories, with quite unremarkable

women as lovers, could be told by the hundreds: of "butch" partners so controlling that they forbid their lovers to attend feminist clubs, gay bars, or even mixed social groups; "egalitarian" lesbian marriages where division of household duties provokes hostile argument; lesbian lovers who so zealously protect a straight image for business reasons that they will shun a partner totally who comes out or is exposed, thus causing heartbreak (and on at least one occasion, suicide); even, as Del Martin and Phyllis Lyon report, instances of sexual incompatibility and frigidity can characterize lesbian unions.

In general, there is absolutely no reason to think that lesbian love is essentially any purer or more spiritual, more refined or wholesome or honest, less potentially exploitative or conflict-ridden, than heterosexual love; no reason to think that a lesbian orientation is necessarily more emotionally healthy than a heterosexual one; or that loving women holds less potential for causing pain than does loving men.

Lesbianism does not represent any advanced stage of development in the overall progress of emerging feminism. It is not, in personal terms, superior: It is only different. In any personal relationship between two women, it will still invariably be true that one will give more, one take more; one care more, the other take advantage of that caring. (On the banal plane of housekeeping, probably one will be neat, one messy.) As Simone de Beauvoir concluded, "Like all human behavior, homosexuality leads to make-believe, disequilibrium, frustration, lies, or, on the contrary, it becomes the source of rewarding experiences, in accordance with its manner of expression in actual living—whether in bad faith, laziness and falsity, or in lucidity, generosity, and freedom."[13]

Lila:

"Sisterhood Is Powerful–
It Can Kill You"

Lila sits on the edge of her bed, wearing a short black lace negligee. It is six P.M. She has been wearing the negligee all day. In fact, she has been wearing negligees for several days. "Why go out?" she asks. "I haven't been able to think of a single reason."

The last time she did leave was to keep a weekly appointment at Elizabeth Arden: The straight, turned-under style she occasionally chooses is now being taken over by rebellious curls. She's not wearing her characteristic silver eyeshadow and tawny blusher which dramatize her dark complexion. "Why bother with makeup? I can't think of a single reason."

Lila is also not bothering with meals (she has lost eleven pounds during the two weeks of her almost-total self-imposed "retreat" in this disordered, expensively furnished apartment she calls Tara), errands, (she has not picked up a new Cacharel shirt being held for her at Bloomingdale's), women's movement business (she's not going to the Halloween hex on a local TV channel, though it was she who unearthed the discrimination figures and suggested the hex demonstration), or writing (she has an eighty-page outline for a novel due one month from now, but why bother? She'll think about it tomorrow. . . .)

Right now, she'll be polite to an unannounced visitor and explain the new lines of sharing and communication she has established with her cat, Morgan.

"Morgan really understands me very well. In fact,

Morgan's consciousness has been way ahead of mine all along. Morgan always understood that there was no reason to go rushing around trying to change the world. Morgan always knew it was cozier just to spend days in bed and rest up from memories of past lives. Morgan has had eight, I've only had one past life, but it's enough to rest up from, I'll tell you!"

"Now, Morgan," Lila suddenly picks up the placid animal and shifts her position to sit cross-legged on the bed, her back against the pillows, "if *you'd* show some initiative, I would too. It's all your fault," she gently scolds the cat, "if I sit around all day. You just do nothing but set me a bad example. But then—oh hell, who needs an activist cat?"

Lila has been spending her days reading novels, chain-smoking, and thinking—"You know, putting things together in my own head the way you only can in solitude."

One thing she wonders about is martyrdom.

"The city is full of martyrs. It fascinates me. Why do women give up comfortable lives, and jeopardize jobs to throw themselves like lemmings into some cause or other. I've asked four of five women what's so important about divorce reform, or women in sports . . . or the quota system. Not one of them can really tell me *what* makes them do it!"

Lila has really asked that question of herself, turning inward, trying to find some answer. She herself qualifies as a movement martyr: Four years ago she was a successful insurance underwriter married to a successful businessman, and had a three-story house upstate. Three years ago she had a high-paying job as advertising director for a black cosmetics firm. Then she was hostess of a lively, much-talked-about morning talk show, "Listening In With Lila."

"Then I got into media reform."

Lila gradually turned against a sexist system that was offering her some sort of low-magnitude stardom. It was Lila who organized the Image of Women committee, collecting hundreds of "defamatory ads showing sexy ladies curled around Scotch bottles or auto tires"; Lila who set up a monitoring network for identifying sexist TV ads; Lila who, as an offshoot of her attack on the "Fly Me!" ads, aided the organization of Stewardesses for Women's Rights.

It was Lila who filed the first license challenge for sexism, and who retrenched to fight the extended license renewal act that "the pigs in Congress tried to use as a roadblock against us," Lila who went after a trade regulation ruling for affirmative disclosure on vaginal deodorant sprays.

It was also Lila's idea to enlist other media organizations in the feminist fight against unfair programming and employment practices. "Jesus, three months ago you should have seen me! I was a windup doll: calling press conferences, cajoling speakers, lining up panels, on the phone to every news desk in this fucking city, *and* on top of that I had to get this brilliant inspiration that the way to keep the Establishment from playing off the feminists against the blacks and the Puerto Ricans was to line up *with* other minorities; so my committee met with the Puerto Rican Media Alliance and the Black Citizens for Fair Media. What a fiasco.

"The game plan was good. The problem was that any given station would tell us, 'We'd like to help you ladies, but we're involved in doing things for the racial minorities right now'; then turn around and tell the black and PR groups, 'Sorry, but we're trying to adjust our employment practices to include more *women.*'

"Both PRMA and BCFM agreed, somewhat suspiciously, to meet with us; but when I made the reasonable suggestion that we draw up a joint quota request based on current employment figures in the urban area, the PR representative said, 'Wait a minute; that's unfair because the Puerto Rican population is underrepresented in the employment statistics,' and the black representative said, 'Oh no, it's blacks who are the last hired and first fired, and whose unemployment is greatest,' and furthermore, see, nobody could agree on whether to use a black lawyer, a Puerto Rican lawyer, or a feminist lawyer! Now I ask you, *how* are you supposed to fight white male supremacy under *those* conditions?"

That failed coalition attempt wasn't Lila's only disappointment.

Briefly: Lila's media committee sought and received a five-thousand-dollar grant for media research; the check was sent to national NOW earmarked for Lila's committee. Somehow weeks went by and the check was not given to Lila. Months went by and her inquiries were not answered. Finally Lila phoned the foundation that had awarded her the funds. An astonished foundation officer set up a conference call immediately with a NOW national officer and Lila. "We're afraid we're going to have to return your check," the NOW officer told him. "A *committee* cannot seek foundation money without national approval."

Undaunted, Lila promised to resubmit the proposal "with twenty-four hours if it can be managed" as a chapter project rather than as a national project.

"That cannot be done," calmly replied the NOW offi-
cial, "according to policies which specifically forbid any
chapter committee from soliciting funds without authoriza-
tion from the *national* task force whose programs coordi-
nate with those of the chapter committee."

"Holy fucking Christ," thought Lila, "before I can get
any work done, do I have to change the bylaws?"

"Don't think you've heard the last of this," she said
aloud into the telephone, and hung up muttering, "Sisterhood! Fuck . . ."

That night, key members of Lila's chapter gathered at
her house to begin a strategy plan that would last five
months: a Chapter Rights committee was declared, on an
emergency, *ad hoc* basis; a first draft of a Chapter Bill of
Rights prepared; a delegate from the committee appointed
to request a hearing before the National NOW board,
which would meet in Washington, D.C. in February 1974,
two months prior to the national convention in Houston;
and contacts with other chapters were reviewed with a goal
of gathering support for the Chapter Rights movement at
the convention (Denver was fairly independent. . . .
Helen Goldman from Houston could be counted on. . . .
What about Boston? . . . What about Chicago. . . ? What
about Lucy Davis in Detroit?) A memo and questionnaire
were drafted inviting all other NOW chapters to share their
feelings on this issue. And one thousand buttons saying
"Chapter Rights" were ordered.

It all seemed quite a while ago, Lila yawned: the
nights in Houston spent rousing delegates along the corridors of the Rice Hotel; the floor fight following the general session when a coalition involving the committee on
Image, Law, and Employment had managed to remove the

entire Chapter Rights issue from the board agenda. . . .

Even longer ago, of course, was Lila's initial introduction to women's movement politics.

The introduction seemed an unlikely one. Lila was at the time the stereotype of what movement women would have called a "corporate cupcake," of which the prototype was considered to be Helen Gurley Brown—a woman who had risen within a corporation in part by plying feminine wiliness, exploiting her uniqueness as a female within an otherwise almost totally male power structure.

Lila had a large home serenely distant from the city, a husband whose own career success was notable even in that achievement-oriented community, a small son, a live-in maid, and—*almost as an afterthought*—a career at Friends' Insurance Company as an underwriter. "My job is *not* my life, I'm not a hyperachieving type," she explained whenever the suggestion was raised that she might be. She was always out of her office at four-thirty, in fact, and home in time to bathe (in *Joy* or *Chanel*), change into something pretty, and spend some time alone with the baby while the maid prepared dinner. She and her husband often went out in the evenings, too, and if Lila was a little bit late for work sometimes because of this, it simply didn't matter. Her husband Ben sometimes grumbled as *he* got out of bed at eight-fifteen and saw her turn over and set the alarm ahead another hour, "Why is it *I'm* the only conscientious one in this family?" and she'd say something about "My female privilege, dear, if I lost my job it wouldn't count. . . ." And that more or less typified Lila's dedication to the work ethic. Nevertheless, just because of an almost careless brilliance, she was the recipient of several merit awards and a lot of praise, particularly after a

training program she designed and edited for a new sub-
sidiary of the company.

Lila never could quite explain why she'd suddenly, in
late 1971, got around to realizing that her work situation
contained an element of inequity. Since she had been given
the job of assistant underwriter, she had realized she was
performing the functions of a full underwriter, but at the
lower of the two pay scales. She wasn't motivated by
economic necessity, certainly, or by any sudden shift of
attitude toward her that might have been sufficiently pa-
tronizing to produce a private rebellion. Nor was her rebellion instigated by any other woman of her acquaintance
within the firm, and it wasn't caused by *Born Female* or any
of the other books delineating injustices in businesses, because she hadn't read any of the books! "I don't know . . . I
just got a bee in my bonnet one day, I guess," she explains
in a soft southern accent. And on that day she sent a memo
to 120 higher-level women employees at Friends', charting
what she knew to be pay differentials between them and
men in the same jobs.

It was a casual gesture, without a lot of thought behind
it. Most of her life gestures had been similarly casual.

Had she thought about it, she might have predicted
the result: She was summarily dismissed by Friends', without notice, within twenty-four hours. She drove home in her
Alfa, almost entirely unconcerned. She was unconcerned,
too, with her husband's chagrin. Didn't she realize, he
wondered, that they had just made a down payment on a
farm in upstate Connecticut, and could not possibly meet
the payment schedule on his income alone? Was she prepared to let the farm go? Didn't she realize that a private
school for Timmy had been arranged, the maid given a

raise, the Alfa scheduled for overhaul, the summer-vacation cottage in the Bahamas already rented for next summer, with a sizeable deposit paid in advance?

Retroactively, Lila pretended, sipping prettily on her martini (while the maid scurried about the room pretending to be bringing fresh ice to the bar but actually only curious about this rare quarrel), that it was in fact her desire to make more money, a salary rightfully due her, that had prompted her action. This pretense made such sense to her that she began to turn rationalization to reality; her husband's face became less flushed. He asked, more calmly, if she had any reason to think her effort would have been successful. "A memo," he pointed out, "is a brash way to ask for a raise, particularly if it's distributed to one hundred and twenty different people."

"But darlin'," Lila said, "that's the way the woman from NOW *told* me to do it—be straightforward, she said, 'cause the law is bound to be on my side."

"What's NOW?" Ben asked skeptically.

"The National Organization for Women, silly," she replied sweetly, breathing a silent prayer that there would be, in fact, a chapter in town that she could call later that week.

"Well, fine, I hope that they can help you see this through," Ben said, mollified at last. They enjoyed a quiet dinner, and the next morning Lila did indeed contact the local NOW office, and was told by a woman named Renee, who answered the phone, that tentatively, yes, they believed they could help her. They hadn't had many class-action suits in this chapter, but other larger and older chapters had, and they'd investigate and see if they couldn't use some legal approach to stand behind her and any other Friends' women employees who might want to join a suit for equal pay. Convinced that she had a right to expect help, Lila returned to her office, demanded from the branch manager the right to use her telephone and former office for a two-week period, since her employment agreement had guaranteed her two weeks notice in case of dismissal. And, with a vague threat of NOW action if there was any trouble on the question, got him to agree.

Lila used the two-week period, of course, for the sole purpose of organizing women employees to demand their rights. For the first time, she felt she experienced overt discrimination—for the first time, she wasn't a "cupcake" anymore.

But by becoming something of a feminist and something of a fighter for equal rights at last, Lila had acted with the presumption that the organization that was meant to back such fights would stand behind her. It was with more than casual disappointment that she took the message, hesitantly delivered by Renee, that NOW could not back her case, for reasons that she, Renee, did not clearly understand but which might have something to do with the fact that NOW was seeking, and had a good chance of receiving, a sizeable grant from Friends' for a pending CILE project.

CILE was a set of initials Lila was to become much more familiar with before her history in the movement reached its zenith, but at the time she did not even inquire what the initials stood for: She just said, "Well, there are always other jobs," cleared her personal accessories from her desk, and walked out of her office for the last time.

But there weren't, as it turned out, "always other jobs," for Lila found employment directors cool—despite her impressive record at Friends'. She quickly concluded that she might be facing an informal blacklist initiated by

Friends', which, through its subsidiaries and a tight personal information system, controlled about 80 percent of
insurance in the state and which had labeled her as a trou-
blemaker. Since her only experience was in underwriting,
it seemed unlikely that she could switch fields without accepting a much lower salary, and every job opening she
sought out *in* the underwriting field seemed blocked.

With her husband's consternation deepening into bitterness, Lila decided to try to fight for support within
NOW, and took a simple, predictable tactical step: She
wrote to officials at state, local, and national levels, outlin-
ing her situation, pointing out the logic of support for her
case and the good it would do for the movement to win its
first major class-action victory against a major corporation.
Her friend Renee threatened to quit working for the local
NOW office if Lila's case was not backed by an *amicus*
brief—and was finally (months later) forced to make good
on her threat. Getting more serious about the matter, Lila
(going against her husband's wishes) hired her own lawyer,
and became a bit more frightened and worried by what now
loomed more and more as an inevitability: NOW, for good
or poor or no reason, would not support her suit against
Friends'. Weeks dragged into months; Lila had left
Friends' in January of 1972, and in April of that year she
found herself forced to write an offset letter to all NOW
officeholders of her acquaintance. The letter, in full, is an
impressive plea for feminist justice; in part, it reads as
follows:

> I marvel at the number of letters on my desk from my
> sisters in NOW, and from affiliated women's organiza-
> tions and *ad hoc* groups which may be fighting for such
> unrelated goals as the right to free abortion but who yet,
> hearing of my case, took time to write me of their . . .
> feelings of support. . . .

I also marvel at the fact that my phone seems never to stop ringing. Three times this evening . . . I have received calls from women telling me they are "with me" and wish me the best. . . . From such outpouring of expression, I can only conclude that my case not only holds potential for becoming a *cause célèbre* but is *recognized as being a vital test case of equal rights for women in the area of sex discrimination in employment.*

I am, however, deeply distressed by a strange dichotomy of feeling and action. Verbal support is offered to me —tangible support is not. . . .

Thus I have begun to react to verbal affirmations of support with an uncharacteristic skepticism: I have begun to ask those of you who write and call, *"Why . . .* will you not support me with promise of an *amicus* brief?" The answers I have received so far are by no means satisfactory. I have received no good reasons, only poor excuses—excuses such as "The time may not be right," "There are tactical reasons for seeking a test case with a less formidable company," "I can't for personal reasons," "I can't because no one else has done so yet." . . . In sum, the feeling seems to be that while my case has validity, it is *just another case* and not sufficiently compelling to justify personal or organizational risk. . . .

Mine is not "just another case." Mine is not just another instance wherein "just another company" is subjecting "just another woman" to sex-based salary inequity. The company which dismissed me is both large and well-respected and has taken some pains to project an image of beneficence, fairness, and liberalism ("You have a Friend at Friends"). A unified feminist approach in support of my case could expose and end such hypocrisy not just within this one insurance company ("just another

*insurance company") but make other major corporations
in all job fields aware that the women's movement is
serious, principled, unified, and not to be trifled with.*

Are we serious about sex discrimination? *Are* we principled? *Can* we unify? If the answer to these questions is a
rousing "yes," we can speed the end of sex discrimination. If the answer to these questions . . . falters, then
we must ask to what extent the principle of expediency
has permeated the cause of justice for women. My action
at Friends' was a simple one, one of a woman seeking
justice. . . . I should be exceedingly surprised to find
myself a sacrificial lamb. I call on my sisters *not* to let this
happen. Remember ours is not "just another cause."

.In sisterhood,

A few days later, in a handwritten note to a woman
who would the following year be a powerful figure on the
national NOW board, Lila wrote,

I intend to pursue my sex discrimination case to the
finish. . ... and so do NOW members Renee and
[Norma]. . . . But there will be problems. . . . In part
due to my efforts during my final two weeks at Friends',
a West Coast Friends' woman's caucus was organized,
but it's being sabotaged by NOW out there, and I believe I know why: [Name] of LDEF has been active in
trying to stifle my case, and [Name] is a personal friend of
[Lydell Pearsons], Friends' board chairman. I repeat, I
intend to pursue my case to the finish—assuming, of
course, my health holds out.

It didn't. Lila suffered a nervous breakdown before
her letter reached her friend, and when she emerged from
the hospital six weeks later, she found herself faced with a
request for a legal separation from her husband, who also
wanted custody of the child and subsequently won it.

She moved to New York City, found a roommate recommended by her friend Renee, and—given her native wit, attractiveness (and brilliance)—found that she could choose from among several "glamour" jobs offered by the expanding job market of that time.

"The only catch was . . ." that since her new roommate was an active NOW member ". . . why the shit I was so stupid as to do something like *that*" Lila began to attend the New York NOW meetings ". . . and why the fuck I didn't see that I'd end up tangling with CILE again . . ." and began to care about media reform, quickly taking leadership of the important but languishing media image committee, investing it with a powerful personal magnetism, building its effectiveness even as she tore down, once more, her renewed store of personal energies.

"Christ, though, how could you *not* care about the garbage the media gives us, especially in the ads. . . ." She gestures toward the wall of her apartment, where such ads as Fieldcrest and Black Velvet scotch are taped to the wall. She is cradling Morgan. The Fieldcrest ad says,

Mother, for a while this morning, I thought I wasn't cut out for married life. Hank was late for work and forgot his apricot juice and walked out without kissing me, and when I was all alone I started crying. But then the postman came with the sheets and towels you sent, that look like big bandanna handkerchiefs, and you know what I thought? That those big red and blue handkerchiefs are for girls like me to dry their tears on so they can get busy and do what a housewife has to do. Throw open the windows and start getting the house ready, and the dinner, maybe clean the silver and put new geraniums in the box. *Everything to be ready for him when he walks back through that door.*

"I mean Christ, how can any woman *not care* about being so manipulated into images—so distorted and unfair, distorted and gross . . . yes, using the grossest of all stereotypes for the mean purpose of upping the Gross National Product. . . ." (smiles, pleased with that, then frowns again) "I mean, *how can any woman not care?*

"Do you realize," she challenges, "how dependent the woman of the 1970s is upon the media for her concept of herself? Do you realize how distorted the concepts are she receives? Jesus, like a fun-house mirror. . . .

"Look," she explains, as though delivering a speech, "despite the fact that forty-two percent of all women are in the labor force, the media show women almost exclusively as housewives, mothers, or sex symbols, obsessed with shiny furniture and sanitized playroom surfaces, the right bra and toothpaste, or whiter-than-white wash or blonder-than-blonde hair. . . . And do you realize how discrimination in *employment* interacts with media discrimination? Look how many decision-making positions in the news media, for instance, are held by men—almost all! Just look at my desk—you'll see!"

And on her desk, on the top of a stack of similar figures, are the statistics for editorial positions on the Washington *Post*, where the ratio of males to females is as follows:

> Managing editors 10/0
> News desk editors 9/0
> Finance and other special sections 9/0
> Metropolitan, national, and foreign desk editors 50/3
> Style section 7/1

"How can any woman *not be active* in the fight? How can any woman *not be involved?* And yet . . . Christ, look what happens when you do care. . . ." Lila is cradling Morgan, and she is crying softly.

(Isn't that the answer to the question you've been asking other women about martyrdom, Lila? You've martyred yourself in a way, just as other women have, because you care so deeply about something that's wrong—so deeply that you have no choice but to try to change it. . . .)

Lila wipes a few tears on Morgan's fur, looks up, lowers her head in a half-nod *yes*, as though she intuits the unspoken thought, but doesn't answer, just repeats her own last phrase, "Look what happens when you do care. . . ." then shifts her posture and is suddenly asleep.

Within a week she will realize that she is on the verge of a second, milder nervous breakdown, will explain with vaguely humorous sarcasm to the admissions psychiatrist at a secluded Maryland hospital, "I want your best shrink, and your fanciest room—maybe the Zelda Fitzgerald room, if anybody remembers. Don't you think first-class treatment will help me deal with being a second-class citizen?" She smiles intently, not sure he's getting the joke. "The reason I want therapy is . . . I'm a feminist, you see." (She pronounces it in an exaggeratedly southern way, as *fiminist*.) "Ever hear the slogan, *Sisterhood is Powerful?* It is, you see. Sisterhood is powerful." She chuckles, "It can kill you. . . ."

Several weeks later, during a relaxed session with her therapist, she will recall that phrase, repeat it, trying to analyze it. "Have I stumbled across something there?"

"Maybe," her physician, a Dr. Laura Henderson, will respond. "It's not that the women's movement operates malevolently. But the mental health field now has, in part thanks to feminism, established ways to help women who've been victimized by *sexism*. We simply don't have any guidelines for helping those women—hopefully few—who've been victimized by *feminism*."

Lila thought about that for a while.

Then, with a determined look both indicative of recovery and predictive of future action, she said, "Well, now, maybe I'll just have to make that a project when I get out of here. . . . maybe I'll just have to do that!"

She gave a broad smile, already planning.

The Search for Status:

Housewife/Volunteer

vs. Woman with a Career

How can a woman earn more money? She has to go
where the men are–in the professions, in
management, in white-collar jobs.[1]

—Caroline Bird

Swinging fringe benefits are the icing on the
employment cake. I'm frankly in favor of bonuses plus
profit sharing plus *a salary that lets you play the*
market, invest in a discotheque, decorate in Ming
dynasty, or buy yourself a Crown Russian sable. I
think it's marvelous that a girl can charge up a
twenty-dollar wash and set when she's on a business
trip. I rejoice for the woman who gives a business
cocktail party in her home and finds herself with nine
opened bottles of Scotch left over. I can't find a thing
wrong with the practice of exchanging business
Christmas gifts when it nets me three gift certificates
from Saks Fifth Avenue. . . .[2]

—Letty Cottin Pogrebin

Work, status, money, fringe benefits. To most
people who have ever lived on this earth, such concepts
would be totally without meaning. In societies other than
our own—particularly before industrialization and speciali-
zation, when one person's work was identical to every
other's—work held no particular aura of desirability. In
primitive societies and in early agrarian societies, skill at
hunting or soil-tilling might be rewarded, but there was no

particular prestige attached to being a hunter or farmer. It's simply what everyone was, or did. The tasks involved were elemental necessities, not ideals linked to concepts of self-worth. Work was not worshipped, had no praises sung to it: It was *tolerated*; it was not pursued as a prize or used as a barometer to determine status.

No one equated work with self-fulfillment; indeed, anyone who bothered with notions of self-fulfillment at all saw work as a barrier to this goal, not an avenue to it!

The money system, and the concept of variable occupations, some of which resulted in more earned income than others, altered that. And in nineteenth-century America the Protestant ethic elevated the concept of economic success almost to the point of deification. Gold amassed on earth would lead to heavenly reward, since God favored industry and achievement. (In a sense, you *could* take it with you.) Early twentieth-century schoolchildren learned about the robber barons along with the poets and thinkers who were their contemporaries—and were often implicitly urged to emulate the robber barons rather than the peculiar poets (there are no Horatio Alger stories with the likes of Emerson or Thoreau as heroes). One's work was one's worth. And this work mystique became a *male* mystique simply because it was men who were assigned the social role of amassing the money.

The female emancipation movement, when it came along, seeking to escape from the feminine mystique, simply adopted the masculine one. The emphasis on economic reward for effort, if not exactly single-minded, is at least unquestioned as a fundamental feminist tenet: Equal Opportunity, Equal Pay for Equal Work, and other such slogans were the messages first to reach us. Leading feminist writers on careers for women, wrote, like Bird and Pogrebin, that to earn money *women have to go where the men are*, without bothering to inquire in any detail as to whether men *liked* it there.

Do they?

Are men really enamored of the work ethic, the dollar value system, the traditional set of "male" priorities and definition of what constitutes meaningful achievement? A fifty-thousand-dollar-a-year "man" is adjudged by society to be more valuable than his twelve-thousand-dollar-a-year assistant. Are either of them totally comfortable with that?

Comfortable or not, men of course capitulate to it. Men will ordinarily, if given a choice between two of several jobs, decide which job to take according to the single criterion of salary level (when a man does *not*, it is unusual enough to write a book about: *e.g.*, *Beyond Masculinity*, by Warren Farrell).

The higher paying of the jobs may not really offer a more satisfying life or more pleasant working conditions, but that is not the point. One can always relax, enjoy life, and be happy *later*. First: Prove one's worth, make one's mark, collect one's upwardly mobile, ego-enhancing paycheck.

But it could be argued that this male value system has at its core a set of fallacies, a male mystique based on the work ethic that could be well compared to the feminine mystique based on the principle of nurture, independent of economic reward.

It was all very neat as recently as ten years ago. Men were in offices and factories, creating and producing, women were in homes and shopping centers, nurturing and consuming: men were performing instrumental functions, women expressive ones; men dynamic functions, women passive ones; and so on.* And it *was* artificial and arbitrary and inequitable, and there *was* obviously something wrong; and a need to right the balance somehow *was* evident. And in answer to the great psychic problems posed by arbitrary sex-role divisions in the labor force, along came women's liberation. Along came NOW, with messages of new hope and higher purposes, bringing fresh insights not just to all those tired housewives but to the thirteen million women who were to be found trying to mix the Betty Crocker image with a Florence Nightingale one—as they took juice carts through hospital corridors, answered telephones at community hotlines, taught underprivileged eight-year-olds the alphabet, or hosted fund-raising luncheons for Hadassah or drug-abuse centers or politicians. They were willing to work for the sake of the good being done, not requiring tangible expressions of appreciation beyond "We owe the reality of this new hospital wing to the tireless and inspiring efforts of . . ." and "As I thank the voters of this state I must also express my appreciation to those dedicated women who canvassed my district. . . ." or perhaps just a thank-you form letter in the mail, to be particularly cherished if it had a personal handwritten note somewhere in the margin.

A problem was posed by these thirteen million women: How was the concept of *volunteer work* to be regarded by the liberationists? As a socially valuable answer to the personal problems posed by the isolation of the sub-

*It is true that women filled normally male roles in factories during World War II, but this was seen as heroic sacrifice rather than proof of equal ability. And when the war ended, Rosie the Riveter was pushed (or, in some cases, fled) back into the housewife role, and the jobs were given back to the men who "belonged" in them.

urbs or as just another way in which the talents and energies of women were exploited?

The answer from acknowledged feminist information
sources is clear. Service-oriented voluntarism is condemned by Margaret Adams as "an unperceived area of
peonage,"[3] and sniffed at by Doris Gold as
"pseudo-work."[4]

" *'I am my brother's keeper' is the cautious altruism of
those who are themselves enchained,*"[5] proclaimed Beverly
Jones and Judith Brown in the early and influential publication "Toward A Female Liberation Movement."

Most significantly, the fifth NOW national conference
in 1971 passed a resolution which cautioned women to dis-
tinguish between two types of volunteering: traditional or
service-oriented volunteering was contrasted with political,
or change-oriented, efforts. The first of these is viewed by
NOW as detrimental to improving the status of women, a
mere reinforcement of the existing patriarchal system,
while the second is seen to have positive potential.*

> Traditional service-oriented volunteering has been and
> is the unpaid labor of women [primarily] in the area of
> providing social services. It is the work which, as many
> state, "would not otherwise get done." Essentially this
> type of volunteering is usually person- or situation-
> directed and does not focus on reforming the larger polit-
> ical or economic system. In real terms, it is doing work
> for no salary or no wages, alongside of people who are
> being paid, or instead of people who should be paid, by
> government. . . . Why has NOW taken a position
> against service-oriented volunteering? NOW believes:
> • That such volunteering is an extension of unpaid

An example of approved, political, or change-oriented volunteering
given by this task force report was working for NOW.

housework and of woman's traditional role in the home (such as helper, buffer, and supporter) which have been extended to encompass the community

● That such volunteering reinforces a woman's low self-image by offering work which, because it is unpaid, confers little status

● That volunteerism has been society's solution for those, including but not limited to women, for whom there is little real economic choice.[6]

Volunteerism is thus assumed to be just another aspect of that vast social conspiracy aimed at disengaging women from meaningful participation in the economic system —just another way in which women cooperate to cheat themselves (in this case, of about 14.2 billion dollars annually, that being the dollar value of volunteer duties performed, as estimated by *Editorial Research Reports*.)*

"For women, who most often recruit each other into volunteer assignments, consciousness raising on the meaning of voluntarism is in order,"[7] sternly advises Doris Gold.†

Though the housewife-volunteer may feel the surge of spirit that results from "doing something worthwhile," such is only a sad and touching delusion, in the feminist view, since society as a whole does not affirm volunteer work as

---

*An even higher estimate comes from John Dixon of Washington, D.C., director of the Center for a Voluntary Society, who estimates that volunteerism's "gross national product" now totals perhaps *fifty* billion dollars a year.

†Feminists such as Gold tend to overlook that men do volunteer work too. "When males do it" (*i.e.*, volunteering) "they can be dollar-a-year men in Washington, with power and prestige," is the only sentence in which male involvement in voluntarism is mentioned by *Ms.* in their February 1975 special report on the subject. Surely this narrow stereotype cannot account for all men's efforts. In fact, 30 percent of all volunteers in New York City are men (*all* "dollar-a-year" men?); the Lions Clubs provide eye banks in hundreds of cities, the Shriners

valuable, according to two criteria: First, volunteer work is of low social priority; second, it is done for no pay.

On the first point, the NOW Task Force Report on Volunteerism states:

> NOW believes that where high priorities are given, the "work which would not otherwise get done" gets done! And it gets done by paid employees in a planned and coordinated manner. It is clear that neither revenue sharing nor voluntarism has been suggested in such high-priority areas as the development of space technology or in the areas of the military or national defense. How much would have been accomplished in the field of space if the government had asked of its citizens that they volunteer their services, in their free time, and at no pay, to get a rocket to the moon. Are our social problems any less complex or important than a journey to the moon?[8]

But then, not the most agile mental segue or side step avoids the Catch-22 question of *How do we reassign our priorities* so that political and private agencies consider social welfare more vital than technological achievement? *Does this very task not call for reform-volunteer work?*

Further, is it not an almost impossible task to separate service-oriented voluntarism from reform-oriented volun-

maintain Shrine hospitals in dozens more; Rotary, Moose, and Elks Clubs and American Legion chapters have many purely social functions, admittedly, but also perform services of some community value, particularly youth-oriented programs. In an action program called Service Corps of Retired Executives (SCORE), 4,700 ex-executives use their knowledge to help small businesses (one local chapter of SCORE alone created or saved 700 jobs in the slumping city of New Bedford, Massachusetts). A similar group, Active Corps of Executives (ACE) has been set up for the growing number of workers who need on-career help or counseling. Men are also included in Heart Fund, United Fund, and among the number of volunteers (1,594,000 in 1973) who staff 3,177 local chapters of the American Red Cross. And what of Boy Scouts, Boys Clubs of America, Big Brothers?

tarism in terms of real power to effect social change? Is the volunteer who helps Princeton NOW draw up educational-reform guidelines any more powerful than her sister in the Bronx who keeps even one discouraged adolescent from dropping out of school into an unproductive and possibly antisocial existence? To deny the value of the latter seems dangerously simplistic.

To feminism, however, both the housewife and the housewife/volunteer represent reactionary roles: Their activities delay feminist efforts to "obviate notions of maleness vs. femaleness in our society." Adams, for instance, writes,

> The main target of my concern is the pervasive belief (amounting to almost an article of faith) that woman's primary and most valuable social function is to provide the tender and compassionate components of life; and through the exercise of these particular traits, women have set themselves up as the exclusive model for protecting, nurturing, and fostering the growth of others.[9]

Such a "compassion trap," Adams argues, is really an "identity trap" which enables voluntarism to achieve its wide appeal. Community-keeping is only a macrocosmic variant of housekeeping, and ill-equips women psychologically to compete for gain economically. It all, ultimately, gets down to economics. It all gets down to money.

"Money is the root of all power," Caroline Bird declares in *Ms.*; "Surely the making of money is the supreme act of personal power in our society," echoes Doris Gold. "The big bonus of executivehood . . . [is] the monetary comfort which accompanies your rise to a position of some power in the business world," says Pogrebin. Power, it seems, can never be the province of someone who merely begins a reading enrichment program for youngsters, digs a trout pond for the elderly in a southern town, helps ex-convicts, mobilizes neighborhoods to establish recycling centers (or founds Hull House?). Must such volunteer actions really reinforce stereotyped servility, poor self-image, lack of personal power? Are they *really* "pseudo-work"?

In fields of production and service, from advertising to insurance, from assembly lines to laundries, in electronics and biochemistry and computer science, in stores and beauty shops and hospitals, much "pseudo-work" is also involved, surely; and, further, it must be performed according to rigidly prescribed rules and inflexible time-tables.

No flexibility is offered by the seven-to-three hospital shift, the eight-thirty-to-four-thirty factory time clock, or the nine-to-five office job: Hours of arrival and departure are fixed (often with an impersonalizing touch such as a sign-in sheet or mechanical clock-plus-computer card arrangement—or the more human but equally demeaning frown from a superior employee), and job duties are tightly delineated, with adherance to them rigidly enforced.

Does a woman really escape from "pseudo-work," or from what Galbraith calls the "crypto-servant class" *merely because she is paid for work which is essentially servile and routine?* Or does she sense, perhaps, what Charles Reich wrote in *The Greening of America*, that

> Work has become pointless and empty. There is no lack of meaningful projects that cry out to be done, but our working days are used up in work that lacks meaning: making useless or harmful products, or servicing the bureaucratic structures. For most Americans, work is mindless, exhausting, boring, servile, and hateful, something to be endured while "life" is confined to "time off".[10]

Reich wasn't the only complaining voice of the late sixties, of course. In such books as *The Peter Principle, From Those Wonderful Folks Who Brought You Pearl Harbor,* and *The Day the Pigs Refused to Be Driven to Market,* strong dismay at our present system of business ethics, priorities, and structures was communicated (but this type of distress, critical of the very nature of corporations and capitalism, came from men who had been enmeshed in these structures for a while; it was quite different in nature from the criticism of feminists who merely called for "Equal Pay . . .").

If routine jobs offer little to the soul, what about higher-echelon jobs, whose functions rest less on the routinized and which allow for creative effort? Here one would have to be rather Panglossian not to perceive that the paths to "meaningful" career achievement wander through realms of untruth, chicanery, and compromise. On a June morning in 1966 a young graduate, age twenty-four, stood among others who had just received Master of Business Administration (M.B.A.) degrees from Harvard. His father, a toughened but outwardly civilized executive, now nearing retirement, dutifully shook his son's hand and said a few words that summed up the meaning of business in America more trenchantly than any courses his son had taken over the preceding semesters: "You've got lots of principles right now," he said, "and I've got none. And as time goes on, you'll trade your principles for advantages, one by one. And in twenty years you'll be just like me." He chuckled with honest amusement at having the entire system figured out so simply.

Trade a principle for an advantage. How can it feasibly be otherwise? "You've just moved to a new executive position, but already somebody wants your job," begins a rather chilling how-to book called *Survival in the Executive Jungle*.

> The higher your position, the more certain it is that you'll have to fight for it. The hunter who is stalking you as his prey may be one of your subordinates, a "friendly" colleague, or even your boss. In the carpeted upper floors of Executive (Bitter) Suite, the new executive is fair game, without benefit of fair play. . . .[11]

Casual anecdotes tumble over one another in the chapters of this book, competing with one another for savagery. There's the one about the new company man being told, "Sit with your back to the wall, to protect yourself against a knifing. They happen pretty often around here." There's the one about the friendly colleague who will use false "input" to provoke you into disaster, saying, "They want a branch manager who will continue Mr. K.'s basic policies," when they really want an aggressive departure from those policies. There's the character assassin, who says "I personally like Cott, but he's considered controversial." A moment before, no one considered Cott controversial at all; now they will begin to. That's the way it works.

And it is toward just such a world that writers such as Pogrebin beckoned women, touting the superiority of ERA bracelets to engagement rings, recounting alluring little stories of salaries and bonuses and profit sharing and such tidy fringe benefits as the fact that "I had a couch in my office before I had one in my home. The Barcelona cocktail table in my office costs more than we spent for all our dining room furniture put together. My husband and I don't have a single magazine subscription at the house. I bring home twenty-three periodicals which come into my office every month on company subscriptions."[12] And in a discussion of double billing for expenses, which can only be called lighthearted, Pogrebin advises honesty because "Lies are embarrassing to substantiate and almost impossible to remember six months later when the company is up for an IRS audit," but feels it is probably all right to bill your company for taxi fare when you really took a bus or subway, and concludes with "But these are guidelines only. You are welcome to adapt them to your own code of ethics."[13]

Perhaps liberated women ought to be concerned with defining *some* code of ethics, whatever that might be, and communicating it within the corporate community. There's not the slightest bit of evidence that such a trend is building within feminism. Typically, for example, Caroline Bird calls Mary Wells Lawrence "the smashingly successful advertising woman who earned more than $300,000 in 1973 as head of her own agency,"[14] thus applying only the dollar criterion as measure of success, not bothering to ask any questions at all as to how this smashingly successful career was built—whether, for example, the exploitation of unhealthy female stereotypes, which the advertising field typically utilizes, was fought by Wells, uneasily capitulated to, or aggressively developed further—or whether any ethics of business or image at all were adhered to.

Ellen Sulzberger Straus, chairperson of Call for Action, a volunteer agency, in fact felt compelled to write:

> A funny thing happened to NOW on its way to the high purpose of consciousness raising. Following generations of men who have lost themselves in the desert of the work ethic, NOW comes to the rescue of society and winds up worshipping the same almighty dollar. It is sad to see women embrace with such relish one of the arid features of the U.S. life style: the identification of money

as the *ultimate* status symbol, the amount of a paycheck as the only measure of human value. At the same time that many Americans are questioning their "mind-sets," desperately seeking for valid human motivations other than greed, the NOW position implies that the base of human dignity is monetary. It is indeed essential that women become economically independent. But if we limit our sights to that goal alone, if we make of economic independence our sole objective . . . the cost of that journey will be psychic bankruptcy.[15]

The question becomes whether, in adopting the single male/money value system, we are being asked to let any valuable "female" qualities wither through lack of encouragement, or even actively hastening their demise through withholding the light of public focus as to their nature and possible worth.

As women move into fields of business and industry, politics and science, perhaps they ought to bring a few typically "female" principles and preoccupations with them. They ought to ask the social value of the work they are undertaking—not just whether a particular job offers high status and high pay. If this is done, a more sensitive, reality-oriented and humanized system may indeed emerge. But the hoped-for synthesis will not occur if women simply inquire as to salary and fringe benefits.

I personally take small delight in the fact that Mary Wells blithely pays herself a salary of over $300,000. In fact, several of the campaigns for which she has been responsible make me not proud of Mary Wells at all. I am similarly not proud of a woman who develops biochemical warfare material, designs offshore drilling rigs, or acts as apologist for the federal government's position on nuclear energy.

I find it easier to be proud of a professional volunteer than of a "pure" professional. In fact, the willingness of women with professional skills and training—in law, medicine, public relations—to give their time and efforts to worthy causes and individuals for no remuneration, might well be taken as a heartening example by the *un*trained volunteer who has been made to feel somewhat guilty about tossing away hours of her psychic energy.

Typical of thousands of women "professional volunteers" throughout the country is Ann Whitfield, partner in a Gainesville, Florida law firm, who typically has about ninety cases on her books, of which about one-third are either indigency cases or public-interest work. She has filed suits for the Sierra Club, helped develop landscape and flood-plain ordinances, and filed for incorporation for a women's health clinic—and she handles about five nonpaying divorces and custody cases per month. "Obviously I could turn down any case that wasn't fee-generating," Ann admits, "but to me that would be misuse of my legal training. I don't serve the public good by simply merchandising my skills to the highest bidder." I find it easier to be proud of an Ann Whitfield than of a Mary Wells.

The issue of voluntarism seems *central* to the question of women's liberation, since it is a mark of true autonomy to be able to choose one's activities, and spend one's time, according to a set of personally satisfying values. It's simply not enough for women to insist on their share of status and recognition in job and career fields: *They have to ask what that status and recognition represents.* If what it represents does not merge with personally held values, then it is better rejected in favor of nonpaying work, or a lower-status job which has positive social impact, even if lower pay.

There ought to be many options open to women, and indeed to men as well: a full-time job or career, certainly, or part-time work, or work at home, or work as a professional or nonprofessional volunteer. One ought to be able, also, to be a housewife without guilt. It seems the grossest of fallacies to contend that work is only worthwhile if you are paid for it.

There is a selflessness involved in giving oneself through work that is very different from the loss of self in, say, panic or neurosis or unthinking conformity or artificially induced sensations. Unlike any of these other forms of loss of self, becoming absorbed in something of genuine interest and worth, one not only gives but gains—and receives heightened awareness and growth that further develops the personality in a distinctive way.

The volunteer can bring an innovative perspective to a situation partly because she is not paid; she has the independence to check the performance of others and have a real impact on society (which might even be seen as a mutual goal of feminism and voluntarism).

Now, particularly, when for the first time in a generation or more the federal government is withdrawing support from many community services, there exist unprecedented opportunities for individuals to exert personalized authority within their communities to solve problems. It can certainly be taken as a healthy sign that *individual citizens* are attempting to define problems and create responses to those problems, rather than passively waiting for the federal government to dole out a "solution" that is necessarily depersonalized due to distance, bureaucracy, and the paternalism inherent in virtually all federal aid programs. Surely the thought of tens of millions of

Americans giving themselves, their time, energy, and money for the public good, is a heartening vision.

And although individual citizen volunteers should obviously include men *and* women, it is women who have, often, the luxury to provide impetus and leadership and definition of program. Even Margaret Mead urges that women take an active role in volunteer services, and reconciles this with her personal vision of liberation. In the August 1973 *Redbook* magazine, she comments:

> Modern young women, I believe, must be willing to back up their commitment to liberation by taking some responsibility for bringing it about. And the opportunity—more realistically, the necessity—for making this the next step exists here and now in every community in the country. . . . We need to think in terms of responsible action now, action that is initiated by those who have the greatest stake in the future. . . . Here, I think, is the opportunity for young women who are immersed in their lives at home. *For there is an immediate need for volunteers who can find out what is really going on, try to salvage what is most essential, devise ways of filling the gaps and, above all, begin to set new styles for community interaction. It is young wives and mothers who have some time to think, time to look around, time to talk with other women about unmet needs in their neighborhood or section of town, and time to take some part in the action.*   [our italics] And I believe that if they would volunteer to work for their communities now, they would find—because they had taken part in making it so—a more welcoming world when their day for self-fulfillment came.[16]

The Roles of Men and Women:

The Personal Solution

"Memo from NOW Media Image Committee to Historians of the Twenty-First Century," Lila had scribbled once in a mood of mordant whimsy. "Please number among the deleterious social consequences of enforced housewifery: burgeoning birth rate; mental anguish for women; depression and low self-esteem; hysterical emotional manipulation of children and spouse; epidemic obsession with macrame; ecological damage due to separation of production centers from homes; 'seesaw' depression-inflation patterns due to compulsive credit-card spending to kill time—scrappy-mindedness!"

A domestic woman is now to be viewed as an anguished, manipulative shrew, a terror in curlers and chenille. A housewife is definitely *not* (as we were wrongly told, among so many lies) a gloriously feminine girl-woman child-mother set like a jewel on satin-pillowed sofas among polished mahogany tables shining in the sunlight streaming through the picture window. And if the one stereotype is as narrow as the other, it is at least necessary to counteract and balance the other. Such counteraction of domestic myth and image is a central purpose of feminism: One major critique of feminism claims in fact that "the women's liberation movement sprang into existence over the issue of housework,"[1] the intent being to combat the misery among housewives that was so frightening it could only be called, by Friedan, "the problem that has no name."

And yet . . . and yet . . . in apartments and houses in

Encino and Westport, in northern Kansas and central Illinois, on Riverside Drive and on East Seventy-Fourth Street, I have talked with women who for periods of time have had no formal occupation or structured ambition outside their homes—women who *seem* content, who *claim* they are content, and whom I believe to be neither liars nor cretins.

There are not many such women, yet there are some; and oddly enough under different circumstances I often feel that I could happily count myself among them— remembering as I do one year when I allowed myself the questionable luxury of living without outside obligations. I did nothing that I can recall that year that was either productive or of noticeable social value (actually I remember principally soufflés, afternoon-long walks in the woods, visits with neighbors—such things as that). Almost certainly I would use that same year of leisure more creatively if I had another chance at it today; but at the time I was a housewife—"just a housewife," as the saying goes—and I recall it as an extremely pleasant interlude, a last guilt-tinged flirtation with an ultimately inappropriate life style.

It ended, of course, that interlude—due in part to imprecations from the women's movement, but due to other stirrings too: for finally I decided in no way does a perfect soufflé help make a better world. And I've felt more valuable since that time, certainly—but no happier. A word which I invariably, oddly, associate with that period of time is "freedom," a freedom I have felt, since, neither in the most envied employment situations nor the most meaningful organizational work. In what role other than the domestic, after all, can one live according to natural rhythm, impulse, whim? In what other role are one's hours almost entirely one's own? It even seems curious, on reflection, that the first book of the modern women's movement presented not a demand for liberation on the part of women writers, or women lawyers or executives, or women factory workers, but *housewives*. It was housewives who envisioned and sought "liberation," and the popular assumption has been that this was because domestic women were farthest removed from self-determination. But perhaps, instead, it was they who conceptualized "freedom" first because they were closer to it.

The problem was that to the extent that freedom existed for the domestic woman, it wasn't used—and unused freedom is ultimately little different from enslavement. It festers, leads merely to disintegration and all the symptoms which the feminists have so aptly described.

Also, since the domestic role is, in orientation, one of giving and serving as defined by various basic tasks, the freedom seems peripheral: The *work* of giving and serving is at the core. Yet both the nature of giving and serving and the peripheral freedom lead to a central and unarguable point—as Margaret Mead has said, it is the domestic woman who has the time to take an incisive and clear-headed look at the community around her, and thus perhaps better than others see and define social problems. Thus the domestic role seems unique in that it can easily integrate with services subsumed under the label *volunteer*, services undertaken from free will and choice, based on perceived need rather than legal and economic obligation. And this is so not only for practical reasons (lack of prior structured demands on daily time) but because the same qualities of temperament can serve both home and the larger world outside the home.

The ideality, or myth, of both housekeeper and community-keeper are similar; and like most myths they contain some small core of truth. There *are* individuals whose inclination is to give and serve; this *has* proved functional; it *is* to be thought that society finds it handy to rely on someone to take Christmas baskets to the needy and set up neighborhood recycling centers. The fact that the "someone" involved has generally been a woman is perhaps not incidental.

Such activities on the part of women both conformed to and contributed to the assumption that the nature of women differed from that of men, being gentler and more generous. As Cyril Connolly wrote, in a simple statement that might today be read with jaundiced eye alert for hints of patrician condescension, "When every unkind word about women has been said, we still have to admit that they are nicer than men."[2]

Nicer . . . *nicer*. Ah yes, I think we *are*. (Are? Were? *Should be?*)

But if that entire perception or presumption was in any way accurate—if women *are* (were/should be) nicer than men—then perhaps certain leaps of feminist logic are off in altogether wrong directions. Perhaps, as one small example, we ought not to fight to get women *out* of domestic situations but rather figure how to get men *into* them, and thus also into the larger social areas of nurture with which domesticity is compatible. *Perhaps the most radical goal we could aim for would not be to "emancipate" women but to retain their orientation to "feminine" stereotype, continue to idealize some few aspects of that stereotype ("Volunteering is beautiful"), and simply seek to add to the number of those urged to conform to that stereotype—urging such conformity not just among women, but among men as well.*

Shorn of false vanities and biological narcissism, the

nurturing principle stands clearly as the province of the female: Caring and care-giving have simply reached higher stages of development in the roles of women. The problem is that female nurturing tendencies have been channeled too narrowly, encouraged to develop almost exclusively within the province of the home and in relation to biological progeny (thus, overpopulation). There is an urgent need to expand this nurturing principle if we are to even hope to conserve the fossil fuels and clean the air, save the dolphins and the wild horses, stop nuclear fission plants and nuclear/arms testing, challenge the CIA and the Army Corps of Engineers, control arms and hunger and population, *in addition to* caring about the aged who have no visitors and the young who receive too little protein.

As the nurturing principle is expanded (melding "female" nurture with "male" world-view) the fallacy of such feminist statements as " 'I am my brother's keeper' is the cautious altruism of those who are themselves enchained"[3] emerges, and the nihilism (or chauvinism) of such words as

> We do not have in mind the rising price of food, the panic on Wall Street, or Dr. Kissinger's shufflings to keep the world "in balance." We do have in mind the powerful resurgence of the Feminist movement . . .[4]

come clear as well.

Such statements are unconscionable. Even if the validity of every feminist goal, from equal pay to equal orgasm, were to be acknowledged, it would still have to be admitted that feminism is simply not the only drama on earth! Just what will equality between the sexes mean if the "panic on Wall Street" leads to total economic collapse? If widespread starvation leads to nuclear war? If the oceans fill with oil and the air with tritium?

One often hears that feminism, to be justifiable, must be, and is intended to be, a movement of *humanism*, but *globalism* is an equally vital adjunct. We must feel not only an obligation to be our brothers' keeper and our sisters' keeper, but keeper of politics and planet as well—and in a way which is not inconsistent with certain traditional, now oft-denigrated "feminine" qualities and frames of reference.

Currently, masculine models predominate in virtually all political and economic centers of the world. And it is almost a cliché that our present muddled world systems, ridden with malaise and conflict, result from characteristic "male" patterns of behavior. R.S. Willett describes the syndrome:

> The problems with the masculine imposition of structure . . . are all too evident. . . . "Games" and "strategies" are pursued in business and politics, with immense waste of energy and loss of real purpose. Abstract structures are mistaken for reality, metastructures imposed on the original abstractions. The whole male-dominated world shows symptoms of a progressive removal from the *real* world. . . . The faulty abstractions imposed by men on the real world condition decision-making.[5]

Aggressive male behavior in business and politics might be said to typify Western values, which have held technological and industrial development, for example, as worthy goals in and of themselves—with little thought for possible effect on quality of life or consequence to human spirit. By contrast, the "feminine" orientation is thought to be both more cautious and more concerned with the harmonious, characterized by a reluctance to design systems or take actions which might bring injury rather than improvement.

The equity of allowing females to participate in power situations has been pointed out: The *nature* of the participation they could bring, and the synthesis that might result, have been little speculated upon, however. Bernard does comment,

> I view . . . with the same horror as others the raped and ravished earth that has been the natural and inevitable outcome of unbraked male values. The mentality of men created the technology that has made lunar exploration possible, affluence feasible, and the masterpieces of the arts creatable. But it has also led to the violated earth. . . .

and asks "What would have been the outcome for science if women had had more influence on the direction our culture has taken?"[6]

Modification of "unbraked male values" seems urgently needed. Bernard's hope is that a constructive synthesis may occur: Once women do assume power within the current system, they may show an ability, based on their prior orientation, to change that system. Such is a comfortable hope and perhaps a not unrealistic one—for whether of not differences between male and female are caused by genes or by conditioning, *at present* the feminine dynamic is vastly different from the masculine one. As Farrell explains simply, "Men's upbringing treats conflict and combat as the all-important processes of life. This is their reality. Women's upbringing treats growth as all-important. The humane value is clearly growth."[7] (The stereotype of the one might be Richard Daley; the epitome of the other, Rachel Carson.)

But the influx of women into the power establishment cannot be expected to counter insensitive "male" policies *if women are simply urged to adopt the values of the status quo*. And this applies with equal force to areas of politics and science and work and love and leisure.

What is to happen, for example, when women are in a power position which holds potential for international conflict and killing? Is Bernard's implicit hope that women will exert a modifying influence supported by evidence thus far? Unfortunately it seems that placing women in a position of power does not automatically guarantee peace, as evidenced by Indira Gandhi of India, Golda Meir of Israel, and Madame Bandaranike of Ceylon. Dr. Edgar Berman comments (with perhaps excessive cynicism) of these three female heads of state,

> As females, they are no doubt all deeply devoted to peace, so it's probably just coincidental that one of them has just completed participation in her second war in six years (the last as chief of state), another has recently finished a highly satisfactory war of liberation, and the third has been on the verge of civil war twice.[8]

Handed a heritage of male-caused power conflicts, women in power positions have yet to demonstrate clearly that they automatically provide urgently needed checks to male aggressiveness. The temptation, in fact, in this transitional period, may be for women who assume power traditionally reserved for males to "prove" their ability to emulate traditionally masculine modes of exercise of power rather than trying, with equal energy, to preserve the more nurturant and conciliatory qualities that have until now been considered the proper functional province of the "weaker sex."

The broad social goal of course is to alter role prescriptions for men and women, integrating the best traits of both sexes, and rejecting that which is empty reflex or harmful compulsion. In effect, the wisest of the reformers seem to be seeking to achieve a male/female model not unlike that of Eastern philosophy (though not necessarily Eastern practice) which involves the concepts of *yin* and *yang*. The concepts provide a useful analogy, even if in nonscientific vocabulary. *Yin* is an intuitive principle, *yang* an active principle which translates feeling and perception into outward action (or, conversely, yang might be viewed as the active impulse which needs control by the principle of wise insight). Each individual is a potentially complete unit, and must find a balance between the two principles. Social dictates and prescriptions which tell women that they "should have" qualities only of perception and passivity, and which instruct men that they "must be" aggressive, distort the principles of balanced but fluctuating differences (often represented by the following symbol)

into a rigid structure that denies development of part of the personality, a structure that might be visually portrayed as

The attempt of feminism seems to be, however, to eliminate or recondition women away from formerly acculturated qualities, and to produce an almost totally masculine (yang) model:

To anyone who might consider that our culture is already suffering from an overdose of yang, the attempt seems oversimplified and ill-considered, and in fact the ultimate surrender to sexism—a grotesquely wrong attempt to cure the evils of male chauvinism by emulating male values, and in the process losing "feminine" qualities in which pride might rightfully be taken.

Perhaps far more emphasis should be placed on modifying the male stereotype. It is possible that the female provides a better model for the future than the male.

This view was expressed at an early feminist conference by Roxanne Dunbar:

> I want to make a couple of points. One is about this assumption on the part of many people that men are persons and that women want to become persons like men are already. I do not agree with this. What I am talking about is creating a new human being. In comparing the present state of male and female in the world, and particularly in our own society, the female is the better model for the future than the male. . . . I do not want to see women simply accept the male model. We have to go beyond that. . . . we have to talk about *female consciousness.*[9]

Later at that conference, Margaret Mead asked, "So the idea would be that, in the future, men would become as much like women as possible, is that right?" and Dunbar replied in the affirmative. To make men "as much like

women as possible" is of course as irrational a goal as trans-
forming women into "counterfeit men," if we assume we
are pursuing the other-sex stereotypes (the undiluted
stereotypes of male and female would resemble, on the one
hand, a bully, and on the other, an infant—both terribly
unsuited to a complex world). But to win men to adopt the
best functions of the "feminine" is a justifiable goal, and
one whose achievement clearly depends upon a reaffirma-
tion and further development of what Dunbar would call
"female consciousness," rather than abandonment of such
components of that consciousness as nurturance and emotional support.

It is both ironic and disturbing that the women's liberation movement, in its major information sources, is not
seeking to develop female consciousness or reinforce
female values, but is instead seeking to *abandon* female
patterns. Confronted with an admittedly destructive male-
female role dichotomy, feminism seeks to co-opt masculine
structure; and radical feminism envisions an androgynous
structure which is also (in all spheres but the economic)
clearly patterned on the masculine model. The results are
not always those which would have been predicted, or
wished for—following feminist injunctions can distort,
rather than enrich, the lives of women.

Madeline provides a clear case in point. Her problems
in a domestic role were many: poor self-image, lack of perceived social value, poor sex life, unsatisfying motherhood,
boredom. Her life, however, prior to her curious "emancipation," was at least integrated. Seduced by movement
literature which conveyed only fragmentary ideology (em-
phasizing sexual equality principally) and by an explosively
emotional conference on sexuality, Madeline abandoned a
traditional role in favor of a life style so one-dimensional

that it is difficult to predict her reaching anything other than a dead end.

The same is true for many other women who follow feminist admonitions in good faith and seek to graft politically "correct" abstract ideas onto personal lies. Sonia, pursuing some image of freedom or fulfillment, attempted to copy the male prerogative and achieve an equal right to extramarital affairs; Rona sought love from other women, but encountered other women who co-opted the male perspective and treated her as a sex object. Lila's experience brings into sharp focus the controversy regarding a "political solution" vis-à-vis a "personal solution" to instances of injustice. Deserving higher pay, she unwittingly chose a political means of demanding it, with disastrous results. It seems that a certain rare combination of social vision, psychic energy, and self-denial is required to win political solutions which do not yet exist in a general way. (On a personal level, Lila would have done better to quietly ask for a raise. The feminist impatience with personal solutions stems from the fact that such an act would have taught Lila's company no lessons, given other women employees no benefits. Logical enough, but the human cost is sometimes left out of the feminist equation.)

Only Sammie, of the women overviewed in this book, has achieved a seemingly problem-free, workable equilibrium; but she's done so by a departure from the traditional so radical that it is almost unique: In effect, she's defined her own special, separate universe where the existence of men is all but unacknowledged. The problem for the Sonias and the Lilas—and for many, many other women—is that they are attempting to adopt values that are at variance with their conditioning; attempting to cancel out much, if not all, of what they were taught to be. There seems a need to define some transitional phase, and raise some pointed questions during that transition.

Even Shulamith Firestone admits the need for some transitional breathing time in terms of establishing new sexual and life-style norms: "It is unrealistic," she contends,

> to impose theories of what *ought* to be on a psyche already fundamentally organized around specific emotional needs. And this is why individual attempts to eliminate sexual possessiveness are now always inauthentic. We would do much better to concentrate on altering the social structures that have produced this psychical organization—allowing for the eventual—if not in our lifetime—fundamental restructuring of our psychosexuality.[10]

That prescription is certainly being followed. Social structures and economic structures are being altered through such methods as legislation, class-action suits, affirmative action plans. The disappearance of the exclusively domestic woman is hinted at by the essay "The Politics of Housework" by Pat Mainardi and shared-housework contracts in *Ms.*, and even more strongly forecast for the future by textbook reform. (Today, first-graders cheer the achievements of Billie Jean King and Valentina Tereschovka, whereas our hearts were warmed by no one more ambitious than Dick and Jane's mom.) Changes in personal relationships are being brought about by consciousness raising and media reform, and further predicted by vocabulary changes: We are advised even now that one's lover should be called one's *attaché*, the human pronoun changed from *he* or *she* to *te*; that *monohabitation* offers unfettered self-fulfillment; that what we've known as marriage is more precisely to be defined as the *pathological-psychological-interdependent-couple syndrome.*

Conservatives may anticipate such changes with regret, but the changes seem inevitable, and not solely because of any compelling logic or revolutionary fervor on the part of feminists. If the voices of expert sociologists are not sufficient to tell us that increasingly depersonalized institutions are the inevitable result of increasingly complex and overcrowded societies, then either logic or intuition should lead to precisely the same conclusion. The fact remains, however, that it is the women of the future who will reap the results of such alternations as are now beginning. To women today belongs the prerogative of a transitional age: We may aid reform efforts, quietly cling to past norms, forge some personal synthesis, or simply live through the revolution.

Of course "living through the revolution" carries some potential for censure. Movement women scorn this option as "remaining on the plantation" rather than taking the train north; they denigrate women who prefer traditional modes of life as socially irrelevant anachronisms. There is also a potent school of thought which insists that no one *can* sit out a revolution—by not participating, one is in effect choosing sides.

Yet must we all become ardent feminist revolutionaries or movement women? Must we all be stonemasons in the building of this brave new genderless society? What of those women who prefer the flaws of nuclear family life to the more novel dilemmas of the Madelines and Sonias and Lilas? What of the women who feel that an attempt to mind-wrench or brainwash or consciousness-raise themselves out of past conditioning will carry a serious risk—the risk that the supposedly temporary disruptions created by such a process may in fact disorient the personality for a lifetime? Perhaps the answer is obvious: Until the "restructuring" process Firestone speaks of occurs, the women's movement is in fact not one for *all* women but for *some* women.

Let those who will or can put their lives—their life energies and life roles and life styles—on the line. For some, it will not work just yet. For some, the goal of economic affirmation is uninspirational; the idea of household contracts merely tedious; monohabitation, autosexuality, and other adventures of emancipation incompatible with inner impulse. For some, spouse-surrogates are simply not enough. For some, priorities are simply different, and the changes in priorities and life patterns that feminism calls for cannot be achieved without great psychic cost.

Those who, by reason of personal orientation, are reluctant to support the women's movement, need not necessarily make guilty apologies for the regressive nature of their choice. It is even possible, in fact, that reluctance to support the movement at this time can have a positive effect—that of forcing the movement into sharper focus, clearer planning, more careful definition as to just what advantages "emancipation" offers women and society.

Does a world in which instantaneous nuclear conflict is possible need another 50 percent of its population urged to become more aggressive? Will it benefit economies characterized by overproduction of the countless wasteful products of affluence to suddenly find additional numbers at the doors of employment centers demanding five-figure salaries and "swinging fringe benefits"?* Does a society in

*In fact, new environmentally-based economics deem it wise not that women achieve *higher* salaries, but that men accept *lower* ones.

which alienation has become a major problem need an organized campaign against love? These are uncomfortable questions, but an insistence that they be answered by feminist and radical feminist leaders might bring about a new texture to the women's movement—a philosophy of revisionism, not revolution.

Such questions may seem to imply a cautious philosophical retreat to an unsatisfactory past—a past in which women were subjected to injustice and exploitation. Yet it is far too simple to interpret a retreat to tradition as mere philosophical cowardice: Many women who are committing themselves to traditional life styles are making a temporary commitment only. They realize that the traditional, domestic role assigned to females is neither equitable nor totally satisfying, but they also see the failure of feminist leaders to integrate the philosophy of liberation with a satisfying personal life style and a humane world-view. To many it seems that women's liberation is bringing not relevant solutions, but only different problems.

Creating new roles for women is no easy task, but the transition might be aided by a quiet insistence on the part of women that future roles are best built on foundations that already exist—foundations such as the nurturing and supportive components of female orientation and upbringing. Such foundations, compared to those of the masculine character—achievement, production, destruction, ego-aggrandizement—seem far to be preferred, far better suited to help human societies retain their human-ness amidst the mechanized surroundings and mindless bureaucracies of an absurdly "modern" age.

Several social critics have, of late, argued for a retention of the female quality of nurture (Erik Erikson and

Jessie Bernard come to mind) and for its expansion beyond biology. Erikson, for example, believes that ". . . the energies which so far have been primarily concentrated on nurturing and on maternity can certainly be widened to apply to collective things, to a kind of vision of the world."[11] But perhaps this view is expressed most cogently by playwright Myrna Lamb: "Arbitrary sex roles train one body of us to murder, and another body of us to mother. But really—we can all mother—*the world and each other*, and we can murder murder, if we dare. . . ."[12] Could there be any better purpose on this crowded, threatened planet, for women—and for men?

Notes

WHAT IS FEMINISM?

[1] Bonnie Kreps, "Radical Feminism," *Radical Feminism* (New York: Quadrangle/New York Times Book Co. 1973), p. 239.

[2] Simone de Beauvoir, *The Second Sex* (New York: Alfred A. Knopf, Inc., 1953), p. xx.

[3] Betty Friedan, *The Feminine Mystique* (New York: Dell, 1964), p. 13.

[4] Ibid. p. 333.

[5] Catherine Breslin, "Waking Up From the Dream of Women's Lib," *New York* (February 26, 1973), p. 31.

[6] Friedan, op. cit., p. 364.

[7] Lisa Hobbs, *Love and Liberation* (New York: McGraw-Hill, 1970), p. 9.

[8] Ti-Grace Atkinson, *Amazon Odyssey* (New York: Links Books, 1974), p. 47.

[9] Valerie Solanis, "S.C.U.M. Manifesto," *Sisterhood Is Powerful* (New York: Random House, 1969).

[10] Joreen, "Bitch Manifesto," *Radical Feminism*, op. cit., pp. 50-51.

[11] Betty Friedan, quoted in "Liberation of Betty Friedan" by Lyn Tornabene, *McCall's* (May 1971), p. 140.

[12] Betty Friedan, "We Don't Have to Be *That* Independent," *McCall's* (Jan. 1973), p. 18.

THE SEARCH FOR SEX

[1] Mary Jane Sherfey, M.D., "A Theory on Female Sexuality," *Sisterhood Is Powerful* (New York: Vintage Books, 1970), p. 220.

[2] Dana Densmore, "Independence from the Sexual Revolution," in *Radical Feminism* (New York: Quadrangle/New York Times Book Co., 1973), p. 116.

[3] Alix Shulman, "Organs and Orgasms," *Woman in Sexist Society* (New York: New American Library, 1972), p. 292.

[4] Anne Koedt, "Myth of the Vaginal Orgasm," *Radical Feminism*, op. cit. p. 111.

[5] Sally Kempton, "Cutting Loose," *Esquire* (Oct. 1973), p. 251.

[6] Shulman, op. cit., p. 293.

[7] Sheila Cronan, "Marriage," *Radical Feminism*, op. cit., p. 215.

[8] Anselma Del'Olio, *Ms.* (Spring 1972).

[9] NOW Women's Sexuality Conference, Transcript (June 9-10, 1973), p. 14.

[10] Andrea Dworkin, quoted by Richard Goldstein, "Scenes from a Sex Conference," *Village Voice* (October 17, 1974).

[11] Bonnie Kreps, "Radical Feminism," *Radical Feminism*, op. cit., p. 239.

[12] Jane Sorenson and Edythe Cudlippe, *The New Way to Become the Person You'd Like to Be*, (New York: David McKay, 1973), p. 13.

[13]Eibl-Eibesfeldt, *Love and Hate: The Natural History of Behavior* (New York: Schocken Books, 1974), p. 152-53.

[14]Shere Hite, *Sexual Honesty* (New York: Warner Paperback Library, 1974), p. 66. Copyright © 1974 by Shere Hite.

[15]"Lilith Manifesto," *Women: A Journal of Liberation* (Fall 1970).

[16]Jane O'Reilly, "The View from My Bed," *Ms.* (April 1973), p. 54.

[17]Nora Ephron, "Women," *Esquire* (July 1973) p. 42.

[18]Ingrid Bengis, *Combat in the Erogenous Zone* (New York: Bantam, 1973), p. 164.

[19]Sylvia Plath, "Daddy" from *Ariel* (New York: Harper & Row, 1961), p. 50.

[20]Carolyn See, *MOMMA Newsletter* (January 1, 1973), p. 12.

[21]"Masochism," *Viva* (January 1975), p. 108.

[22]NOW Women's Sexuality Conference, op. cit., p. 10.

[23]Shere Hite, op. cit., p. 3.

[24]Ibid., p. 40.

[25]William Kephert, Ph.D., "What Should a Man Do if He Reaches Orgasm Before His Partner?" *Medical Aspects of Human Sexuality* (August 1971), p. 12.

[26]Dr. William Masters and Virginia Johnson, *Human Sexual Response* (Boston: Little Brown & Co., 1966), p. 138.

[27]Rollo May, *Love and Will* (New York: W.W. Norton & Co., 1969), p. 75.

EMOTIONAL FREEDOM

[1]Laura Marholm-Hansson, *Modern Women* (London: John Lane, 1896), p. 183.

[2]Emma Goldman, "The Tragedy of Women's Emancipation," *The Feminist Papers* (New York: Bantam, 1973), p. 514.

[3]Lisa Hobbs, *Love and Liberation* (New York: McGraw-Hill, 1970), p. 2.

[4]Carolyn See, *MOMMA Newsletter* (January 1, 1973), p. 13.

[5]Shulamith Firestone, *The Dialectic of Sex* (New York: Wm. Morrow & Co., 1970), p. 143.

[6]Ibid., p. 145.

[7]Beverly Jones and Judith Brown, *Toward a Female Liberation Movement*, pamphlet (New York: New England Free Press, 1968).

[8]Caroline Bird, *Born Female* (New York: Pocket Books, 1969), p. 208.

[9]Kate Millett, *Sexual Politics* (Garden City, N.Y.: Doubleday, 1970), p. 37.

[10]Ti-Grace Atkinson, *Amazon Odyssey* (New York: Links Books, 1974), pp. 44-45.

[11]Sheila Cronan, "Marriage", *Radical Feminism* (New York: Quadrangle/New York Times Book Co., 1973), p. 216.

[12]Katie Sarachild, *The Newsletter* (May 1, 1969).

[13]"The Feminists, Charter, August 8, 1969," *Radical Feminism* (New York: Quadrangle/New York Times Book Co., 1973), p. 374.

14Jones and Brown, op. cit.

15"Wraparound," *Harper's* p. 102.

16Firestone op. cit., p. 259.

17Karen Durbin, "Casualties of the Sex War," *Village Voice* (April 1972).

18Ingrid Bengis, *Combat in the Erogenous Zone* (New York: Bantam, 1973), p. 162.

19Richard and Anna Maria Drinnon, Eds., *Nowhere at Home: Letters from the Exile of Emma Goldman and Alexander Berkman* (New York: Schocken Books, 1975), p. 161.

THE LESBIAN CONNECTION

1Delores Klaich, *Woman Plus Woman* (New York: Simon and Schuster, 1974), p. 24.

2Anne Koedt, "Feminism and Lesbianism," *Radical Feminism*, (New York: Quadrangle/New York Times Book Co., 1973), p. 250.

3Sidney Abbott and Barbara Love, "Is Women's Liberation a Lesbian Plot?" in Gornick Moran, *Woman in Sexist Society* (New York: New American Library, 1972), pp. 609-20.

4Klaich, op. cit., p. 24-25.

5Ibid., p. 116.

6Del Martin and Phyllis Lyon, *Lesbian/Woman* (New York: Bantam, 1972), p. 116.

8Abbott and Love, op. cit.

9Judith Hole and Ellen Levine, *Rebirth of Feminism* (New York: Quadrangle/New York Times Book Co., 1971), p. 241.

10Klaich, op. cit., p. 212-14.

11Ernest Hemingway, *A Moveable Feast* (New York: Scribner's, 1964), p. 119.

12Nigel Nicolson, *Portrait of a Marriage* (New York: Atheneum, 1974), p. 129.

13Simone de Beauvoir, *The Second Sex*, (New York: Bantam Edition, 1952), p. 399.

THE SEARCH FOR STATUS

1Caroline Bird, *Everything a Woman Needs to Know to Get Paid What She's Worth* (New York: Bantam, 1974), p. 13.

2Letty Cottin Pogrebin, *How to Make It in a Man's World* (New York: Doubleday & Co., 1970), p. 208.

3Margaret Adams, "The Compassion Trap," Gornick Moran, *Women in Sexist Society* (New York: New American Library, 1972), p. 555.

4Doris B. Gold, "Women and Voluntarism" Gornick Moran, op. cit., p. 535.

5Beverly Jones and Judith Brown, "Toward a Female Liberation Movement", pamphlet, (New York: New England Free Press, 1972), p. 32.

[6]*NOW Task Force Report on Volunteerism* (1971).

[7]Gold, loc. cit.

[8]*NOW Task Force Report on Volunteerism*, op. cit.

[9]Adams, op. cit., p. 556.

[10]Charles Reich, *The Greening of America* (New York: Random House, 1970), p. 8.

[11]Burger Chester, *Survival in the Executive Jungle* (New York: Collier Books, 1966), pp. 15-19.

[12]Pogrebin, loc. cit.

[13]Ibid., p. 206.

[14]Bird, op. cit., p. 87.

[15]Ellen S. Strauss, "In Defense of Unpaid Labor," *Ms.* (February 1974), p. 87.

[16]Margaret Mead, "A Next Step in Being a Woman," *Redbook* (August 1973), p. 38-39.

THE ROLES OF MEN AND WOMEN

[1]Midge Decter, *The New Chastity* (New York: Berkley Medallion Books, 1973), p. 19.

[2]Cyril Connolly, *The Unquiet Grave* (New York: Penguin Books Edition, 1967), p. 39.

[3]Beverly Jones and Judith Brown, "Toward a Female Liberation Movement," pamphlet (New York: New England Free Press, 1972), p. 32.

[4]Lila Karp and Renos Mandis, "Genderless Sexuality," *Woman in the Year 2000* (New York: Arbor House, 1974), p. 250.

[5]R.S. Willett, "Working in a Man's World; the Woman Executive," in Gornick Moran, *Women in Sexist Society* (New York: New American Library, 1972), p. 528.

[6]Jessie Bernard, *Women and the Public Interest* (New York: Aldine-Atherton, 1971), p. 41.

[7]Warren Farrell, *The Liberated Man* (New York: Random House, 1974), p. 21.

[8]Dr. Edgar Berman, *The Politician Primeval* (New York: Macmillan, 1974), p. 94.

[9]Annals of New York Academy of Sciences, Vol. 175, Article 3, 1970.

[10]Shulamith Firestone, *The Dialectic of Sex* (New York: Wm. Morrow & Co., 1970), p. 273.

[11]*Time* (March 17, 1975), p. 88.

[12]Myrna Lamb, *The Mod Donna* (New York: Pathfinder Press, 1971), p. 28.